Make-Ahead
MEALS

100+ Recipes for
Home-Cooked Meals
You Can Serve at a
Moment's Notice

VICTORIA SHEARER

SELLERS
PUBLISHING

19 2/81

Dedication
To my wonderful daughter Kristen,
this one's for you!

Published by Sellers Publishing, Inc.

Text © 2011 Victoria Shearer
All rights reserved.

Sellers Publishing, Inc.
161 John Roberts Road, South Portland, Maine 04106
For ordering information:
(800) 625-3386 toll free
Visit our Web site: www.sellerspublishing.com • E-mail: rsp@rsvp.com

ISBN: 13: 978-1-4162-0622-4

Library of Congress Control Number: 2010933889

10 9 8 7 6 5 4 3 2 1

Printed and bound in China.

CONTENTS

INTRODUCTION

The in-laws announced they are arriving on Thursday for the weekend. You just finished a round of golf and your husband invited the rest of your foursome over for a quick bite. You're invited to a potluck supper Friday night and you have to work until 6 p.m. It's your turn to bring the treats for your preschooler's snack-time and you forgot. If any of these frightful scenarios are even slightly reminiscent of your life, you may need a culinary intervention.

Back in the 1970s, television's *Brady Bunch* had Alice in the kitchen, serving up home-cooked goodness at a moment's notice. Claire Huxtable, the lawyer mom from the hit 1980s sitcom, *The Cosby Show*, never seemed to be stressed or unprepared at mealtimes, even though she worked all day. Food played a role in the 1990s series *Seinfeld* too, but those folks were single and spent an awful lot of time eating in a diner.

So is it any wonder that the fast-paced environment in which you find yourself in the twenty-first century often makes you feel more like one of the "Desperate Housewives" than the "Iron Chef?" You might think: "I want to serve great meals to my family and friends, but there is no time." "I try not to buy expensive takeout food, but I often have to work late." "I really do like to cook, but weekends are my only free time."

Don't worry. You don't need an intervention. You need a little inspiration ... and a guidebook for paying it forward. *Make Ahead Meals* shows you how, with some advance preparation during your free minutes, to create gustatory magic — more than 100 tasty dishes that you can cook and serve at a moment's notice, with a minimum of effort.

Some recipes you can assemble early in the day or the night before and refrigerate until cooking. Other dishes, once prepared, will keep in the refrigerator for days, allowing you the flexibility of choosing when and where to serve them. You can prepare many of the *Make Ahead Meals* a month or more in advance and store them in the freezer until that unexpected company rings the doorbell.

Look for the following icons to determine how far in advance you can prepare a recipe:

 make in the morning    make up to 1 week ahead

 make and freeze

 indicates that you'll find a handy tip or explanation that relates to that recipe.

From soups, snacks, and drinks, to main courses, tasty sides, decadent desserts, and special sauces, *Make Ahead Meals* invites you to make the most of your precious time: "Cook now, enjoy later!" And to aid your preparation, you'll find a complete inventory of the ingredients, equipment, and supplies used in the recipes in this book as well as a pocketful of helpful culinary tips and some very useful food facts.

So the next time your role in life requires a culinary sleight of hand, turn to *Make Ahead Meals* for a star turn in the kitchen.

Starters

Drinks, Appetizers, and Soups

- Summertime Lemonade
- Watermelonade
- Iced Lemon Sweet Tea
- Garden Water
- Hot Mulled Cider
- Sangria
- Fruity Frozen Wine Slushes
- Planter's Punch

- Apricot Baked Brie
- Smoked Salmon Pizza
- Mushroom Pastry Pinwheels
- Faux Seafood Biscuit Baskets
- Shrimp Mousse
- Asian Shrimp Bites
- Cocktail Skewers
- Dip It! (3)
- Spread It Around (3)
- Chinese Chicken Cups

- Iced Tomato-Melon Soup
- Chilled Zucchini Soup
- Fresh Herbed Cucumber-Yogurt Soup
- Chilled Chocolate-Almond Soup
- "BLT" Soup
- Mushroom Soup
- Pork Wonton Soup
- Chicken Tortilla Soup

Summertime Lemonade

Nothing says summer like a tall glass of fresh-squeezed lemonade. Or try an "Arnold Palmer"— half lemonade, half Iced Lemon Sweet Tea (recipe, page 9).

1½ cups sugar
½ cup water
1 tablespoon grated lemon peel
1½ cups fresh squeezed lemon juice
5 cups water
Mint sprigs

Up to 1 week ahead: Place sugar and water in a medium saucepan over medium-high heat. Bring to a boil, reduce heat to medium-low, and simmer until sugar has completely dissolved, about 2 minutes. Transfer this sugar syrup to a large pitcher.

Add lemon peel, lemon juice, and water. Stir to combine. Refrigerate until cold. Serve over ice in tall glasses garnished with a mint sprig.

My supermarket sells overripe lemons repackaged for quick sale at a mere fraction of the original cost. Because they are so ripe, these lemons are very juicy. When you find a good deal on lemons, juice them and freeze them in 1½-cup measures. Then you can enjoy fresh lemonade any time of the year.

Makes: 8 cups

Watermelonade

Your kids will love this nutritious fruit drink, which is even more refreshing than lemonade and made with much less sugar. Adults like it too! Try adding a splash of rum or peach schnapps to your cooler.

8 cups cubed, seeded watermelon, rind removed, divided

⅓ cup sugar, divided

1 cup water, divided

¼ cup fresh lemon juice

1 slice lemon

Up to 5 days ahead: Place half the watermelon, half the sugar, and half the water in a blender. Puree on highest speed until well blended. Place a strainer over a large bowl. Pour watermelon puree into strainer. Push on puree with the back of a kitchen tablespoon, extracting as much liquid as possible from the puree. Discard remaining puree and rinse strainer. Repeat with remaining watermelon, sugar, and water. Stir in lemon juice. Place in a covered pitcher and refrigerate for 2 hours or until well chilled. Serve on ice with a slice of lemon.

In Mexico, outdoor markets offer pastel-colored fruit waters served from large bee-hive-shaped jars. Called *agua frescas*, the waters make good use of overripe fruit, including pineapple, strawberries, and cantaloupe.

Makes: 8 cups

Iced Lemon Sweet Tea

Only in the South when you order iced tea are you asked, "sweet or unsweet?" This is sweet tea with a twist — the lemonade concentrate keeps it from being too sweet and adds a nice tang to the flavor.

....

½ cup sugar

2 quarts (8 cups) water, divided

2 family-size or 4 small tea bags

¾ cup (6 fluid ounces) frozen lemonade concentrate, thawed

....

At least 2 hours or up to 2 days ahead: Place sugar and 4 cups water in a large nonstick saucepan over medium-high heat. Bring to a boil. Stirring frequently, boil until sugar has dissolved, about 3 minutes. Remove saucepan from heat. Add tea bags and steep tea for 10 minutes. Remove tea bags.

Transfer tea to a large pitcher. Stir in lemonade concentrate and remaining 4 cups water. Refrigerate iced tea. Serve over lemon ice cubes (see 🌀 below).

....

🌀 To make lemon ice cubes: Cut a lemon into ¼-inch slices. Cut each slice into 4 wedges. Place 1 wedge of lemon in each compartment of 3 ice cube trays. Fill trays with water (or lemonade) and freeze until needed.

Makes: 8 cups

....

Garden Water

This showy water is great to serve for a luncheon or dinner party. The fruits and vegetables add an interesting, subtle flavor to the water, changing it from ho-hum to divine.

3 thin slices English cucumber, about 4 inches long

3 thin slices navel orange, cut in half

3 thin lemon slices

4 thin slices peeled fresh gingerroot

3 quarts (96 fluid ounces) bottled water

4 sprigs fresh flat-leaf parsley

At least 1 hour or up to 3 hours ahead: Place cucumber, orange, lemon, and gingerroot slices in a large glass pitcher. Add water and parsley. Stir to mix. Refrigerate until needed. Serve over lemon ice cubes (see 🙂 on previous page).

🙂 Add a handful of fresh blueberries or cranberries for extra color.

Makes: 3 quarts

Hot Mulled Cider

This is the perfect antidote to a cool fall day or a great sipper when sitting beside the fireplace in the midst of a snowstorm.

½ gallon (64 ounces) apple cider
½ teaspoon whole cloves
Dash ground nutmeg
¼ cup brown sugar
½ teaspoon whole allspice
1 (3-inch) cinnamon stick

Up to 2 weeks ahead: Place cider, cloves, nutmeg, brown sugar, allspice, and cinnamon stick in a large nonstick saucepan over high heat. Bring to a boil. Reduce heat to low and simmer, uncovered, for 10 minutes. Pour cider through a strainer into a large heatproof bowl. Discard spices. Serve immediately in ceramic mugs or transfer to a covered container and refrigerate until needed. Serve cold or reheat cider in a large nonstick saucepan over low heat.

Look for fresh apple cider at farmers' markets during apple season in the fall.

Serves: 8

Sangria

Always a hit at summer outdoor parties, this fruity sangria recipe can be doubled or tripled to serve a crowd. The drink should be made one day ahead so that flavors can marry.

1 (750 ml) bottle syrah or other red wine of choice
1 lemon, juiced and strained
1 lime, juiced and strained
1 orange, juiced and strained
¼ cup pineapple juice
2 tablespoons sugar
3 fluid ounces gin (2 shots)
½ cup thinly sliced fresh pineapple
1 cup thinly sliced fresh or frozen strawberries
3 cups ginger ale

One day ahead: Place wine, fruit juices (lemon, lime, orange, and pineapple), sugar, gin, and sliced pineapple in a large pitcher. Stir until sugar is dissolved. Cover and refrigerate overnight.

To serve: Stir strawberries and ginger ale into sangria. Serve in ice-filled tall glasses.

You can substitute equal portions of frozen mixed fruit and berries in this recipe. Also, experiment with using your favorite fruity liqueur, such as peach schnapps or apricot brandy, instead of the gin or replacing the ginger ale with 7-Up, Squirt, or another lemon-lime soda.

Serves: 8 to 10

Fruity Frozen Wine Slushes

The perfect wine fix on a hot summer day, these slushes are as tasty as they are refreshing. The alcohol in the wine keeps them from freezing completely.

1 (6-ounce) can frozen limeade
1 (750 ml) bottle pinot grigio
1½ cups cranberry juice
1 (750 ml) bottle chardonnay
¾ cup pineapple juice
1¼ cups mango nectar
1 cup peach nectar

At least 1 day or up to 1 month ahead: Place limeade, pinot grigio, and cranberry juice in a blender. Process on low speed for 30 seconds, until frozen limeade is blended with other ingredients. Transfer to a covered container and place in freezer until needed.

Mix together chardonnay, pineapple juice, mango nectar, and peach nectar in a pitcher or large bowl. Transfer to a covered container and freezer until needed.

To serve: Scoop a portion of either wine slush into a tall glass, a margarita glass, or a martini glass. Serve with a straw or sipping spoon.

Experiment with different combinations of juices, nectar, wines, and even fruits to make your own creations.

Serves: A crowd

Planter's Punch

When I lived in the Florida Keys, my dear friend Doc Adams always served a killer planter's punch. He kept his recipe a tightly guarded secret . . . until now. The crucial ingredient is orgeat syrup, a distinctive sweet syrup made from almonds, sugar, and rose water or orange-flower water that is somewhat difficult to find. Substituting almond syrup makes this drink almost like Doc's specialty, but if you can find a bottle of orgeat, grab it. It will last you a lifetime and turn you into your neighborhood's punch specialist.

1½ cups pineapple juice

2 cups orange juice

2 dashes Angostura Bitters

¼ cup (2 fluid ounces) grenadine

1½ cups (12 fluid ounces) white rum

1 tablespoon (½ fluid ounce) Myers dark rum

¼ cup (2 fluid ounces) orgeat or almond syrup

Up to 1 week ahead: Mix together pineapple juice, orange juice, bitters, grenadine, white and dark rums, and orgeat or almond syrup in a large pitcher. Stir to combine. Refrigerate until needed. Serve each drink in a tall glass filled with ice cubes

Orgeat syrup is marketed under the brands of Torani, Fee Brothers, and Teisseire. Doc Adams thinks the French almond syrup is the best (Teisseire), but it is also the most difficult to find and the most expensive. Torani almond syrup is widely marketed in World Market stores and others around the country.

Serves: 8

Apricot Baked Brie

This appetizer will attract your guests like a magnet. It is as showy as it is easy. Be prepared to take a bow for this one.

1 (16-ounce) wheel Brie cheese
⅔ cup apricot preserves, divided
2 tablespoons finely minced jalapeño peppers, divided
½ cup finely chopped pecans, divided
1 ready-to-bake baguette bread

Up to 6 hours ahead: Cut Brie in half horizontally, through the center of the wheel of cheese. Place bottom half of wheel (cut-cheese side up) in the center of a large shallow round baking dish. Spread ⅛ cup preserves over cheese. Sprinkle with 1 tablespoon jalapeños and ¼ cup pecans. Place other half of Brie atop preserves, cut-cheese side down. Spread remaining preserves over Brie. Sprinkle with remaining peppers and pecans. Cover with plastic wrap and refrigerate until needed.

To serve: Preheat oven to 350°F. Cut baguette into ¼-inch slices. Place on a baking sheet on an upper rack in the oven. Remove plastic wrap from Brie. Spoon any preserves that may have oozed out of the Brie back on top of the cheese. Place on lower oven rack. Bake both Brie and bread for 10 minutes. Place toasted bread around Brie in the baking dish. Serve immediately.

You'll find your best price for a Brie wheel at your local wholesale club.

Serves: 16 to 20

Smoked Salmon Pizza

Considered a delicacy by many because it is a little pricey, smoked salmon makes a big impact on the hors d'oeuvre table. This pizza is special.

1 Mama Mary's Thin & Crispy Pizza Crust (½ 16-ounce package)
1 (8-ounce) carton whipped cream cheese
½ cup finely minced red onion
4 teaspoons grated lemon peel (from 1 lemon)
2 teaspoons prepared white horseradish
2 tablespoons rinsed capers
4 ounces smoked salmon, cut in small dice
2 tablespoons snipped fresh dill

Early in the day: Preheat oven to 425°F. Place pizza crust on a baking sheet and coat it with vegetable cooking spray. Bake until browned and slightly crisp, about 5 minutes. Remove crust from oven and place on a cutting board to cool.

Meanwhile, place cream cheese, onions, lemon peel, horseradish, and capers in a small bowl. Mix well. Spread cream cheese mixture evenly over the cooled pizza crust.

Place salmon pieces evenly over cheese mixture. Sprinkle dill over the salmon. Cut pizza in quarters with a pizza cutter. Then cut each quarter into 4 thin slices. Transfer slices to a large serving plate and reassemble pizza. Coat the underside of a large piece of aluminum foil with vegetable oil spray. Cover pizza with foil, oiled-side down, and refrigerate until serving.

You'll find Mama Mary's crusts in their own rack, unrefrigerated, in most supermarkets. They have a long shelf life, so they are a great staple to have on hand in your pantry.

Makes: 16 slices

Mushroom Pastry Pinwheels

Puff pastry is light, flaky pastry made from dozens of thin layers of buttery dough. Making it from scratch is a laborious task at best. But luckily puff pastry can be found, ready to bake, in the freezer section of most supermarkets and is incredibly easy to work with, with spectacular results.

1 (17.3-ounce) package puff pastry (2 sheets)
5 tablespoons butter
1½ cups chopped sweet onions, like Vidalia
1 pound baby bella or button mushrooms, finely chopped
1 teaspoon fresh lemon juice
1 tablespoon fruit-flavored honey mustard
⅛ teaspoon Worcestershire sauce
Pinch coarse salt
Freshly ground black pepper
2 tablespoons flour

Up to 1 month ahead: Place puff pastry at room temperature to defrost. Melt butter in a large nonstick skillet over medium heat. Add onions and mushrooms and sauté, stirring frequently, until all liquid has evaporated, about 8 minutes. Stir in lemon juice, mustard, Worcestershire sauce, salt, and pepper to taste. Sprinkle flour over mushroom mixture and cook for 2 minutes more, stirring frequently. Place skillet on a hot pad in the refrigerator to allow mushroom mixture to rapidly cool.

Unroll puff pastry sheets and even out the rectangles with a rolling pin. Spread half the cooled mushroom mixture evenly over each puff pastry sheet. Starting at the short side of each sheet, roll up pastry over mushroom mixture, forming a long log. Press pastry at seam to seal. Roll each log in a sheet of plastic wrap, then cover with aluminum foil. Freeze until needed.

Up to 2 hours ahead: Unwrap mushroom logs and place them on a cutting board to defrost for 15 to 20 minutes. Preheat oven to 350°F. Slice each semi-defrosted mushroom log into ½-inch slices with a serrated knife. Place each slice, mushroom-side down, 2 inches apart on an ungreased baking sheet. Bake for 25 to 30 minutes, until golden. Keep at room temperature until serving.

 Serve as a cracker-type snack or topped with thinly sliced Swiss cheese.

Makes: 5 dozen

Faux Seafood Biscuit Baskets

Imitation crab and imitation lobster are actually processed products made from a white fish called pollock. Less than two percent of the product is actually crab or lobster, but the fish is flavored to taste like the real deal. Imitation seafood is a great cost-conscious substitute, but if your budget is flush enough, use lump crab meat and cooked lobster pieces.

1 (8-ounce) package imitation crab meat, finely chopped
1 (8-ounce) package imitation lobster meat, finely chopped
1 (1.6-ounce) package dry Knorr Alfredo mix
1½ cups milk
1 tablespoon butter
1 teaspoon snipped fresh chives
2 (12-ounce) packages Pillsbury Grands! Junior flaky biscuits
8 ounces fresh mozzarella cheese, finely shredded

Up to 1 month ahead: Preheat oven to 375°F. Mix imitation crab and lobster meats together in a large bowl. Whisk Alfredo mix and milk together in a medium saucepan over medium heat. Add butter and bring mixture to a boil, whisking frequently. Reduce heat to low and cook 2 minutes more, whisking constantly. Whisk in chives. Pour Alfredo sauce over seafood mixture and stir until ingredients are well combined.

Coat a 24-count mini-muffin pan with vegetable cooking spray. Working with several biscuits at a time and keeping the rest refrigerated, divide each biscuit into 3 flat pieces of dough. Stretch dough into a circle. Press each circle of dough into a muffin cup, forming a dough basket. Place a kitchen teaspoonful of seafood mixture into each dough basket. (Basket should be about three-quarters full.) Top with a generous sprinkling of cheese.

Bake for 11 to 12 minutes, until biscuit baskets are lightly browned and cheese is bubbly. Remove from oven and allow them to cool for 5 minutes. Gently transfer biscuit baskets to a wire rack and cool completely. Place in a covered container and refrigerate or freeze until needed. Repeat with remaining seafood filling and biscuits.

To reheat: Preheat oven to 325°F. Place desired number of Faux Seafood Biscuit Baskets on a baking sheet. Bake for 10 minutes, until biscuit baskets have heated through. Serve immediately.

Biscuit dough separates easier if it is cold. Work with only 3 biscuits at a time. Keep the rest covered with plastic wrap in the refrigerator until needed.

Makes: 54

Shrimp Mousse

This updated classic has a little kick to it, thanks to the addition of wasabi mayonnaise. Wasabi is Japanese horseradish, which adds hotness to foods more akin to strong mustard than that of chili peppers.

1 teaspoon olive oil
1 pound medium shrimp (31/40s), peeled and deveined
½ teaspoon lemon-dill seasoning
1 (11-ounce) can Campbell's Tomato Bisque soup
1 (8-ounce) package cream cheese
1½ envelopes Knox gelatin
½ cup cold water
¼ cup wasabi mayonnaise
¾ cup plus 1 teaspoon mayonnaise
1½ cups finely chopped celery
½ cup finely chopped sweet onions, like Vidalia

One to 2 days ahead: Place olive oil in a large nonstick skillet over medium heat. Toss shrimp with lemon-dill seasoning. Stirring constantly, sauté shrimp until they are pink and cooked through, about 3 minutes. Transfer shrimp to a cutting board and finely chop. Set aside.

Place soup in a medium nonstick saucepan over medium-low heat until it comes to a slight boil. Add cream cheese and cook, stirring frequently, until cream cheese has melted, about 3 minutes. Place gelatin and water in a small bowl. Whisk until gelatin has dissolved. Whisk dissolved gelatin into soup mixture. Transfer soup mixture to a large bowl. Stir in the wasabi mayonnaise and ¾ cup regular mayonnaise.

Add chopped shrimp, celery, and onions to bowl. Toss until ingredients are well combined.

Grease a 5½-cup decorative shrimp or fish mold with remaining 1 teaspoon mayonnaise. Transfer shrimp mixture to mold. Cover with plastic wrap and refrigerate.

To serve: One hour ahead, carefully slide a knife around edges of mold. Invert mold onto a serving platter. When mousse releases onto platter, remove mold, cover mousse with plastic wrap, and refrigerate until needed. Serve with bite-size crackers.

Be sure to allow plenty of time for the mousse to release from the mold. Because of the density of the mousse, it doesn't release as quickly as a Jell-O mold does.

Serves: A crowd

Asian Shrimp Bites

Taking the time to assemble these shrimp logs really pays it forward. You'll have appetizers in the freezer for multiple occasions.

1 pound medium shrimp (31/40s), peeled and deveined

⅓ cup minced scallions (about 3 large)

3 tablespoons snipped fresh cilantro

½ teaspoon ground ginger

2 tablespoons soy sauce

1 teaspoon Asian sweet chili sauce

1 egg, separated

½ cup chopped water chestnuts

1 (17.3-ounce) package frozen puff pastry (2 sheets), thawed in refrigerator

1 teaspoon white sesame seeds

1 teaspoon black sesame seeds

Plum-Ginger Sauce (recipe, page 132)

Up to 1 month ahead: Place shrimp in food processor and pulse until coarsely chopped. Add scallions, cilantro, ground ginger, soy sauce, chili sauce, and egg white. Pulse until ingredients are well combined. Transfer to a medium bowl. Stir in water chestnuts.

Unfold 1 sheet puff pastry atop a large sheet of parchment paper. (Store remaining pastry sheet in refrigerator until needed.) Roll pastry with a rolling pin into an oblong measuring about 11x13 inches. Cut pastry in half lengthwise with a pizza cutter, so that you have 2 pieces, each 5½x13 inches. Place egg yolk in a small bowl and whisk with 1 tablespoon water. Set aside.

Place one-quarter shrimp mixture in a line along the uncut long pastry edge, leaving about 1 inch pastry uncovered at each end. Fold in pastry at each end and carefully roll pastry over filling, forming a long, cigar-shaped log. Dip a clean finger into egg wash and coat underside of pastry seam to seal edges. Transfer pastry log to a large parchment paper–lined baking sheet, seam-side down.

Repeat process with remaining pastry dough so that you have a total of 4 long logs. Using your finger, coat top and sides of shrimp logs with egg wash. Mix white and black sesame seeds together in a small bowl. Sprinkle a quarter of the seeds over each log. Place baking sheet in freezer for 4 hours, until logs are completely frozen. Wrap each in plastic wrap, then wrap all the logs together in plastic wrap and return to freezer until needed.

To serve: Remove desired number of shrimp logs from freezer and place on a parchment paper–lined baking sheet to thaw at room temperature. Preheat oven to 400°F. When logs have thawed (about 45 minutes), bake for 25 to 30 minutes, until puff pastry is golden and shrimp filling has cooked through. Remove from oven. Allow shrimp logs to cool for about 10 minutes, then slice into bite-size pieces. Place on a serving platter, pastry-side up. Drizzle with Plum-Ginger Sauce. Insert a toothpick into each appetizer. Serve with extra sauce on the side.

This recipe makes 4 logs, each about 12 inches long. You'll get about 15 pieces per log, so you can defrost what you need and have great appetizers on hand with very little work involved.

Serves: A crowd

Cocktail Skewers

Two of Italy's most favorite starters appear together in a star appearance on these skewers. Taste the ingredients on one end and you'll enjoy a bite of prosciutto and melon. Eat the offerings on the other end and you'll savor a tiny caprese salad — mozzarella, basil, and tomato.

½ cantaloupe, seeded and scooped with a melon baller
1 (3-ounce) package thinly sliced prosciutto, cut into ½-inch strips
1 (8-ounce) container miniature mozzarella balls (about 25)
3 large fresh basil leaves, cut into 1-inch strips and strips cut in half
25 to 30 small grape tomatoes
Salt and freshly ground black pepper

Early in the day or 1 day ahead: Assemble ingredients on 4-inch wooden cocktail skewers. Skewer 1 melon ball. Fold up 1 strip of prosciutto and thread it onto the skewer. Add 1 mozzarella ball to the skewer, then a basil piece, and finally a grape tomato. Place in a large covered container. Repeat with remaining skewers until all ingredients are used. Cover container and refrigerate until needed.

To serve: Place skewers on a serving plate. Season with salt and pepper to taste. Serve at room temperature.

You'll find the miniature mozzarella balls in the deli cheese section of your supermarket. They are often called mozzarella bocconcini or mozzarella ciliegine.

Makes: 25 to 30

Dip It!

DAFFODIL DIP

Closely guarding her secret vegetable dip recipe for decades, my friend Barbara finally disclosed this tasty combination for discerning make-ahead cooks. But how the dip got its name must remain a mystery.

1 (8-ounce) package cream cheese, softened at room temperature
½ cup mayonnaise
½ cup snipped fresh flat-leaf parsley
1 hard-boiled egg, finely chopped
2 tablespoons minced sweet onions, like Vidalia
1 clove garlic, minced
Salt and freshly ground black pepper

Up to 1 week ahead: Place cream cheese, mayonnaise, parsley, egg, onions, and garlic in a medium bowl. Stir until all ingredients are well combined and mixture is creamy. Season with salt and pepper to taste. Cover and refrigerate until needed. Serve at room temperature with fresh vegetable crudités, such as baby carrots, pea pods, sliced jicama, and broccoli florets.

Makes: 1¾ cups

CHEDDAR-PEPPER DIP

White cheddar cheese and roasted red peppers marry in this piquant dip, reminiscent of the Southern favorite, pimento-cheese.

4 ounces cream cheese, softened
1 cup shredded extra-sharp cheddar cheese
¼ cup sour cream
¼ cup mayonnaise
½ cup chopped roasted red bell peppers (from a jar)
2 teaspoons hot sauce
⅛ teaspoon salt
2 pieces bacon, cooked crisp and crumbled
⅓ cup thinly sliced scallions

Up to 3 days ahead: Place cream cheese, cheddar cheese, sour cream, mayonnaise, roasted peppers, hot sauce, and salt in a food processor. Process until smooth. Transfer to a covered container. Fold in bacon and scallions. Cover and refrigerate until needed.

To serve: Place in a small serving bowl. Serve at room temperature with breadsticks.

Makes: 2 cups

COCONUT-CURRY GUACAMOLE

You'll find prepared guacamole in the produce section of your supermarket. I use Yucatan brand, which is packaged in four 2-cup pouches. Commonly found at Sam's Club stores, it can be frozen for months. Pouches defrost in minutes in a bowl of hot water.

2 tablespoons minced shallots

2 teaspoons minced, seeded jalapeño peppers

⅓ cup snipped fresh cilantro

¼ cup plain yogurt

3 tablespoons sweetened flaked coconut

1 tablespoon gingerroot paste or finely minced gingerroot

3 tablespoon fresh lime juice

½ teaspoon mild curry powder

2 cups prepared guacamole

¼ teaspoon salt

Up to 1 day ahead: Place shallots, jalapeños, cilantro, yogurt, coconut, gingerroot, lime juice, and curry powder in a food processor. Process until well blended. Transfer to a medium bowl. Fold in guacamole and salt. Transfer to a covered container and refrigerate until needed.

To serve: Transfer to a small serving bowl and serve with lime-flavored tortilla chips or chilled cooked shrimp.

Makes: 2¼ cups

Spread It Around

Sometimes the best appetizers are your friends' tried-and-true favorites. I twisted a few arms to bring you these three North Carolina favorites.

....

MAJOR GREY'S CHUTNEY-CURRY SPREAD

This one is a major palate pleaser.

....

1 (8-ounce) package cream cheese, softened at room temperature
⅛ teaspoon salt
¾ teaspoon mild curry powder
½ (9-ounce) jar Major Grey's mango chutney
1 slices bacon, cooked crisp and crumbled
1 tablespoon minced scallions

....

At least 1 day or up to 3 days ahead: Place cream cheese, salt, and curry powder in the bowl of an electric mixer. Beat on medium-high speed until fluffy. Line a 1½-cup bowl with plastic wrap. Place cream cheese mixture into bowl and press with the back of a spoon so that cheese mixture conforms to the shape of the bowl. Cover bowl with plastic wrap. Refrigerate until needed.

To serve: Early in the day, remove plastic wrap cover from refrigerated bowl. Flip bowl upside down on a serving plate. Pull on plastic wrap to release cheese. Remove plastic wrap from around cheese. Spoon chutney over the surface of the cream cheese (cut up any large pieces of mango first). Sprinkle crumbled bacon over chutney. Sprinkle scallions on top of mound. Refrigerate until needed. Serve at room temperature with crackers.

....

You can freeze the curry-chutney mound after placing the cream cheese mixture in the bowl. Cover bowl with plastic wrap and aluminum foil before freezing. To serve, remove coverings from top of bowl early in the day. Flip bowl upside down on a serving plate. Pull on plastic wrap to release cheese. Remove plastic wrap from around cheese mound. Allow cheese to defrost to room temperature. Then proceed with layering toppings as described above. Refrigerate until serving.

Serves: 6 to 8

ITALIAN FLAG SPREAD

Let's hear it for the red, white, and green.

2 sun-dried tomatoes, cut in half lengthwise

4 small fresh basil leaves

3 (5.2-ounce) packages Boursin garlic-herb cheese, softened at room temperature

¼ cup prepared sun-dried tomato pesto

¼ cup prepared basil pesto

1 freshly baked French baguette, thinly sliced

Up to 4 days ahead: Line a 2-cup bowl with plastic wrap, then coat wrap with vegetable cooking spray. Arrange the 4 sun-dried tomato halves and the 4 basil leaves in the bottom of the bowl, creating an open flower.

Crumble 1 package of cheese into bowl, pressing firmly with the back of a spoon to form a smooth layer over the flower. Place bowl in freezer to chill. Mix sun-dried tomato pesto with the second package of cheese. Remove bowl from freezer and spread sun-dried tomato-cream cheese mixture over the first layer. Return bowl to freezer to chill. Mix basil pesto with remaining package of cheese. Remove bowl from freezer and spread basil pesto-cream cheese mixture over sun-dried tomato layer. Cover with plastic wrap and refrigerate until needed.

To serve: Remove plastic wrap from top of bowl. Place a serving plate atop bowl and invert bowl onto plate. Remove bowl and plastic wrap and allow the spread to reach room temperature. Surround it with bread slices and serve.

You'll find both sun-dried tomato and basil pesto in your supermarket. Freeze leftover pesto in ice cube trays and use as needed. Three to 4 defrosted cubes equals ¼ cup. Don't use sun-dried tomatoes in oil in this recipe. Look in the produce section of your supermarket for the soft, dried sun-dried tomatoes in a bag.

Serves: 12 to 16

RED SALMON-PECAN SPREAD

Canned salmon never looked or tasted so good!

1 (8-ounce) package cream cheese, softened at room temperature

Dash Worcestershire sauce

Several dashes cayenne pepper

2 tablespoons fresh lemon juice

¼ teaspoon Liquid Smoke

3½ teaspoons grated onion

2½ teaspoons prepared horseradish

¾ teaspoon salt

1 (14.75-ounce) can red salmon, rinsed, drained, flaked, and bones/skin removed

3 tablespoons snipped fresh flat-leaf parsley

¾ cup chopped pecans

One to 2 days ahead: Place cream cheese, Worcestershire sauce, cayenne pepper, lemon juice, Liquid Smoke, grated onion, horseradish, and salt in the bowl of an electric mixer. Beat on low speed until well blended, scraping down the bowl several times. With a rubber spatula, fold salmon into cream cheese mixture.

Line a 2-cup bowl with plastic wrap. Transfer salmon mixture to bowl and press with back of spatula so that mixture follows contours of the bowl. Cover bowl with plastic wrap and refrigerate until needed.

To serve: Early in the day, remove plastic wrap from top of bowl. Place a serving plate atop bowl and invert bowl onto plate. Remove bowl and plastic wrap. Sprinkle parsley over salmon spread, pressing it into spread on all sides. Repeat this process with the pecans. Cover spread and plate with plastic wrap and refrigerate until needed. Serve with crackers.

Be sure to carefully remove backbone vertebrae and all but the very tiny, flexible bones from the salmon.

Serves: 12 to 18

Chinese Chicken Cups

Bite-size but packed with a riot of flavors, these appetizers will be a hit at any party.

2 tablespoons bottled plum sauce

5 tablespoons soy sauce, divided

¾ cup shredded baby carrots

¾ cup thinly sliced red bell peppers (about 1 inch long)

¾ cup sliced scallions

3 tablespoons guava nectar

1 tablespoon sugar

1 tablespoon sesame oil

2 teaspoons cornstarch

1 teaspoon olive oil

1 cup chopped cooked chicken

2 (1.9-ounce) packages frozen Athens Mini Fillo Shells, defrosted

¼ cup Plum-Ginger Sauce (recipe, page 132)

2 tablespoons sesame seeds

One day ahead: Whisk plum sauce and 1 tablespoon soy sauce together in a small bowl. Place carrots, bell peppers, and scallions in a medium bowl. Add plum-soy mixture and toss until vegetables are well coated. Set aside.

Whisk 4 tablespoons soy sauce, guava nectar, sugar, sesame oil, and cornstarch together in a small bowl. Set aside.

Place olive oil in a large nonstick skillet over medium heat. When oil is hot, add carrot mixture and sauté for 2 minutes, stirring frequently. Add chicken and soy sauce mixture and sauté, stirring constantly, for 1 minute more, until sauce has thickened and is syrupy. Transfer to a covered container and refrigerate until needed.

One hour before serving: Fill each shell with chicken mixture, drizzle with Plum-Ginger Sauce, and sprinkle each shell with sesame seeds. Transfer to a serving platter, cover with plastic wrap, and refrigerate until serving. Serve at room temperature.

If you don't have Plum-Ginger Sauce on hand in your freezer, you can substitute 2 tablespoons bottled plum sauce. Since it is more concentrated than the homemade version, place a dollop in the bottom of each fillo shell, then top with the chicken mixture and sesame seeds. You can substitute any fruit nectar for the guava nectar. You'll find the fillo shells in the frozen foods section of your supermarket.

Makes: 24 to 30

Iced Tomato-Melon Soup

Served in crystal glasses tucked into a bowl of ice cubes, this festive summer soup is great for a party buffet.

1 tablespoon extra-virgin olive oil
1½ pounds peeled, chunked cantaloupe
1 cup Fresh Tomato Sauce (recipe, page 56)
1 cup orange juice
½ cup ice cubes
2 tablespoons snipped fresh basil
1 tablespoon fresh lemon juice
¼ teaspoon coarse salt
½ teaspoon cracked black pepper
2 tablespoons snipped fresh flat-leaf parsley
1 tablespoon chopped pistachios
½ tablespoon freshly grated orange peel
¼ cup sour cream
4 sprigs mint

At least 1 day or up to 4 days ahead: Place olive oil in a large skillet over high heat. Add the melon and cook, stirring constantly, until melon releases juices, 1 to 2 minutes. Place melon in blender. Add tomato sauce. Pulse until smooth. Add orange juice, ice cubes, basil, lemon juice, salt, and pepper. Pulse until mixture is smooth. Transfer to a covered container and refrigerate overnight to marry flavors.

To serve: Mix parsley, pistachios, and grated orange peel together in a small bowl. Puree cold soup once again in blender. Place each serving in a small crystal glass. Top each serving with 1 tablespoon sour cream. Place ½ tablespoon pistachio mixture atop sour cream. Fill a large bowl with small ice cubes. Place each glass deep in the ice cubes. Place a mint sprig between glasses on the ice. Allow diners to serve themselves.

This recipe makes about 5½ cups. Double or triple the recipe if you are serving a large number at a buffet supper.

Serves: 6

Chilled Zucchini Soup

Elegantly presented in crystal champagne glasses, this chilled soup imparts a surprisingly spicy jolt to the taste buds. Serve the soup accompanied with several Faux Seafood Biscuit Baskets (recipe, page 18) for a substantial first-course offering.

5 thin zucchini, unpeeled and thinly sliced

1½ teaspoons salt, divided

½ cup chopped onions, like Vidalia

¼ cup jasmine or basmati rice

2 cups College Inn Thai Coconut Curry Broth

1 cup chicken broth

2 teaspoons snipped fresh dill or ¾ teaspoon dried dill

½ teaspoon curry powder

1 teaspoon Dijon mustard

1 cup half-and-half

At least 3 hours or up to 1 month ahead: Place sliced zucchini in a large colander and sprinkle with 1 teaspoon salt. Allow to sit for 20 minutes. Rinse zucchini with cold water and drain well. Squeeze out extra liquid by handfuls and transfer zucchini to a large soup pot. Add onions, rice, broths, dill, ½ teaspoon salt, curry powder, and mustard to pot. Place pot over medium-high heat and bring to a boil. Reduce heat to low and simmer for 20 minutes, stirring occasionally.

Transfer zucchini mixture to a blender. Hold a kitchen towel over top of blender (so hot liquid does not splatter and burn you), and pulse blender until ingredients are chopped, then puree until smooth. Transfer to a covered container. Stir in half-and-half. Refrigerate until needed. (See 🌀 below about freezing the soup.)

To serve: Place each serving in a champagne glass and serve with a long-handled spoon.

🌀🌸 If you want to freeze the soup, do not add the half-and-half until you are ready to serve it. Or, serve half the soup (stir in ½ cup half-and-half) and freeze the other half (without half-and-half).

Serves: 8

Fresh Herbed Cucumber-Yogurt Soup

This is a great cold soup to serve on a hot summer day when you can find a plethora of fresh herbs at your local farmer's market. Serving the soup in martini glasses adds a little pizzazz!

2 cups plain nonfat yogurt

2 English cucumbers, peeled, quartered lengthwise, and cut into ½-inch slices (4 cups)

1 teaspoon garlic paste or finely minced garlic

2 teaspoons snipped fresh mint leaves

2 teaspoons snipped fresh dill

1 tablespoon snipped fresh chives

1 tablespoon honey

½ teaspoon salt

⅛ teaspoon white pepper

2 tablespoons chopped roasted pistachios

At least 1 day or up to 3 days ahead: Place yogurt, cucumbers, garlic, mint, dill, chives, honey, salt, and pepper in a blender. Puree until smooth. Season soup with additional salt and pepper to taste. Transfer to a covered container and refrigerate until needed.

To serve: Stir soup, then ladle 1 cup into each of 6 martini glasses. Sprinkle 2 teaspoons chopped pistachios atop each serving.

You can find English cucumbers (1-foot-long and shrink-wrapped) in your supermarket all year long. At the height of the fresh produce season in the summer, look for small, thin cucumbers at your local farmer's market. They will have only tiny, edible seeds and will be just as sweet and crunchy as the English cucumbers.

Serves: 6

Chilled Chocolate-Almond Soup

Who says chocolate is not one of the basic food groups? Chocolate-aholics may want to devour this cold soup as a brunch entrée, but it also makes a sensational dessert.

1 (5-ounce) package Jell-O Cook & Serve chocolate pudding
4 cups (1 quart) half-and-half, divided
⅓ cup Crème de Cocoa
2 tablespoons Amaretto
⅓ cup slivered almonds
⅓ cup unsweetened coconut

At least 1 day or up to 2 days ahead: Place pudding mix in a 3-quart nonstick saucepan. Pour in 3 cups half-and-half and whisk until well combined. Place saucepan over medium heat and cook, whisking constantly, until mixture comes to a boil, about 4 minutes.

Remove saucepan from heat. Whisk in remaining 1 cup half-and-half and the liqueurs. Transfer soup to a covered container and refrigerate until needed.

Place almonds in a small nonstick skillet over low heat. Toast almonds, stirring occasionally, until golden. Remove from heat, allow almonds to cool, and store them in a small zipper bag at room temperature until needed.

Place coconut in hot skillet over low heat. Toast coconut, stirring constantly, for 1 minute. Remove from heat, allow coconut to cool, and store it in a small zipper bag at room temperature until needed.

To serve: Place about ¾ cup chilled soup in each of 6 decorative glasses. Sprinkle each serving with toasted almonds and coconut. Serve with a small dessert spoon.

Serve the soup in martini, margarita, wine, or other decorative glasses. You can eat it with a spoon or sip it from the glass.

Serves: 6

"BLT" Soup

With all the flavors of the classic sandwich that bears the same initials, this "BLT" is made with bacon, leek, and tomato. Leeks are in the same family as onions and garlic. Their stalks are composed of layers of leaf sheaths. Dirt tends to get caught between the sheaths, so be sure to rinse them thoroughly.

2 tablespoons butter

1 leek, white parts only, washed well, dried with paper towel, and thinly sliced

3 strips center-cut bacon, diced

2 pounds ripe plum tomatoes, peeled, seeded, and diced

1 teaspoon fresh thyme or ½ teaspoon dried

¼ teaspoon onion powder

¼ teaspoon garlic powder

¼ teaspoon salt

⅛ teaspoon black pepper

2 bay leaves

4 cups chicken broth

½ cup heavy cream or sour cream

At least 24 hours or up to 1 month ahead: Melt butter in a large nonstick saucepan over medium heat. Add sliced leeks and diced bacon and cook until bacon is crisp, about 2 minutes. Add tomatoes, thyme, onion and garlic powders, salt, pepper, and bay leaves. Sauté for 5 minutes, stirring frequently. Add broth. Bring to a boil on high. Reduce heat to low and simmer for 20 minutes, stirring occasionally.

Remove bay leaves and puree soup in batches in a blender. (Hold a kitchen towel over top of blender so hot liquid does not splatter and burn you.) Add salt and pepper to taste. Transfer to a covered container and refrigerate or freeze until needed.

To serve: Serve soup cold or place soup in a large nonstick saucepan over low heat until it is warmed through. Drizzle each serving with a little heavy cream or top each serving with a small dollop of sour cream.

Before adding the heavy cream or sour cream, you can freeze this soup in covered containers or pour it into the cups of a maxi muffin tin and place in the freezer. When soup is completely frozen, pop it out of the muffin tin and store in a freezer-weight zipper bag. Each is a single-serving portion. Simply defrost in a bowl and reheat or serve cold.

Serves: 6

Mushroom Soup

This soup is exquisite with ordinary button and baby bella mushrooms, but you can jazz it up with a combination that includes more exotic mushrooms, such as shiitake, cremini, or porcini if you'd like.

1 tablespoon olive oil

2 pounds baby bella and/or white button mushrooms, wiped clean and thinly sliced

1 cup chopped sweet onions, like Vidalia

2 tablespoons fresh lemon juice

2 tablespoons dark brown sugar

1½ teaspoons dried thyme leaves

⅓ cup white wine

1 (14-ounce) can vegetable broth (2 cups)

1 (32-ounce) carton chicken broth (4 cups)

1 teaspoon salt

½ teaspoon black pepper

Busha Browne's Pepper Sherry or cream sherry

Up to 3 days ahead: Place olive oil in a large nonstick skillet over medium heat. Add mushrooms, onions, lemon juice, brown sugar, and thyme. Sauté for 5 minutes, stirring frequently, until mushrooms have softened and any released liquid has evaporated. Add white wine and cook for 5 minutes more.

Transfer mushroom mixture to a large saucepan over medium heat. Add vegetable and chicken broths, salt, and pepper. Bring mixture to a boil, then reduce heat to low. Cover and simmer for 30 minutes, stirring occasionally.

Remove 1 cup mushrooms from soup with a slotted spoon and set aside. Transfer soup to a blender and puree (in batches if necessary) until smooth. (Hold a kitchen towel over top of blender so hot liquid does not splatter and burn you.) Pour soup into a covered container. Stir in reserved mushrooms. Refrigerate until needed.

To serve: Place soup in a large saucepan over low heat until it is heated through. Serve with Busha Browne's Pepper Sherry or cream sherry on the side.

Busha Browne's Pepper Sherry can be found in the condiment section of your supermarket. It adds a spicy jolt along with the sweet distinctive taste of sherry. You can drizzle cream sherry atop the soup instead, if you don't want to tamper with the delicate flavoring of the soup.

Serves: 6

Pork Wonton Soup

No need to eat out at a Chinese restaurant when you have these pork wontons stock-piled in the freezer. Because the wontons go from freezer to broth, it is the ultimate quick soup.

½ pound ground pork

1 tablespoon gingerroot paste or finely minced peeled gingerroot

3 tablespoons snipped fresh cilantro

3 tablespoons hoisin sauce, divided

1 (12-ounce) package wonton wrappers

4 cups chicken broth

1 cup thinly sliced button mushrooms

¼ cup thinly sliced scallions (about 1 large)

4 sprigs fresh flat-leaf parsley

At least 1 day or up to 3 months ahead: Place pork and gingerroot in a medium nonstick skillet over medium heat. Sauté, stirring constantly, until pork has cooked through. Remove pork from skillet with a slotted spoon and drain on paper towels. Place pork in a food processor and pulse until finely ground. Transfer ground pork to a medium bowl. Add cilantro and 2 tablespoons hoisin sauce and stir to combine.

Place 3 tablespoons water in a small bowl. Place I teaspoon (measuring spoon) pork filling in center of 1 wonton wrapper. (Cover other wrappers with damp paper toweling until needed so they don't dry out.) Dip your clean fingertip in the water and moisten all edges of the wonton wrapper. Fold opposite corners of the wonton wrapper together to form a triangle. Press edges to seal. Place in a covered container. Repeat with remaining filling and wonton wrappers, placing a sheet of waxed paper between layers of wontons in the container. Freeze until needed. (Makes 36 wontons.)

To make soup: Place chicken broth and I tablespoon hoisin sauce in a large nonstick saucepan over medium heat. Bring to boil, stirring occasionally. Reduce heat to low. Add 12 frozen wontons. Simmer soup, stirring gently, for 3 minutes. Add mushrooms and scallions and simmer 1 minute more.

To serve: Place 3 wontons in each of 4 soup bowls. Divide the soup (about 1 cup per serving) equally among the 4 bowls. Garnish each with a sprig of parsley. Serve immediately.

You'll have enough frozen wontons to make three batches of soup. Don't worry if a couple of the wontons split open during the simmering process. The pork filling will season the soup and the empty wontons will taste like Chinese noodles.

Serves: 4

Chicken Tortilla Soup

Mexican cooks routinely use up their stale tortillas by making tortilla soup.

10 corn tortillas, divided

2 tablespoons olive oil

2 tablespoons garlic paste or finely minced garlic

1 cup chopped sweet onions, like Vidalia

2 cups peeled, seeded, chopped tomatoes (about 1½ pounds)

¼ cup tomato paste with basil, garlic, and oregano

8 cups chicken broth

2 tablespoons snipped fresh cilantro, divided

1 teaspoon chili powder

1 teaspoon ground cumin

½ teaspoon coarse salt

¼ teaspoon black pepper

3 cups finely diced cooked chicken

Olive oil spray

1 avocado, pitted, peeled, diced, and sprinkled with fresh lemon juice

1 cup shredded sharp cheddar cheese

One day or up to 1 month ahead: Stack 4 corn tortillas. Using kitchen scissors, cut tortilla stack into ½-inch strips, then cut strips into ½-inch pieces. Set aside.

Place olive oil in a large nonstick soup pot over medium heat. Add garlic and onions and sauté for 1 minute, stirring constantly. Add diced tortillas and sauté for 1 minute, stirring constantly. Add tomatoes and sauté for 2 minutes, stirring frequently. Stir in tomato paste, chicken broth, 1 tablespoon cilantro, chili powder, and cumin. Bring to a boil, reduce heat to low, and simmer, covered, for 30 minutes.

Place one-third of the soup in a blender. Hold a kitchen towel over top of blender (so hot liquid does not splatter and burn you), and puree in batches until smooth. Place pureed batches of soup in a large covered container. Season soup with salt and pepper. Add chicken and remaining 1 tablespoon fresh cilantro. Stir to combine. Refrigerate soup uncovered until cool. Cover container and refrigerate or freeze until needed.

To serve: Preheat oven to 400°F. Using kitchen scissors, cut remaining 6 tortillas into strips 2 inches long and ¼ inch wide. Place strips in a medium bowl and coat liberally with olive oil spray. Spread strips on a nonstick baking sheet. Bake for 10 minutes, tossing occasionally with a spatula, until tortilla strips are crispy. Remove from oven and set aside.

Place soup in a large soup pot over low heat. Cook for 15 minutes, stirring occasionally, until soup has heated through. Place crispy tortilla strips, diced avocado, and cheddar cheese in individual serving bowls. Ladle soup into individual soup bowls and allow diners to top soup with condiments of their choice.

 For easy prep, use a rotisserie chicken in this recipe.

Serves: 6

Entrees

Poultry, Meat, Fish and Seafood, Pasta, and Brunch

- Chicken Strudels
- Chicken Tikka Kabobs
- Béarnaise Chicken and Biscuit Pie
- Chicken-Vegetable Parmesan
- Cranberry–Pistachio Stuffed Chicken Breast Salad
- Chicken Saltimboca Roulades
- Tomato-Coconut Chicken Curry
- Turkey Picadillo
- Pizza Potpie

- Meatballs Four Ways
- Greek Meatballs with Mediterranean Sauced Penne
- Thai Meatballs in Red Curry Sauce with Jasmine Rice
- Hawaiian Meatballs in Sweet and Sour Sauce with Coconut Rice
- Sicilian Meatballs in Fresh Tomato Sauce with Spaghetti

- Duck Breasts with Raspberry Port Sauce
- Mustard and Jack Daniels Marinated Sirloin Steak
- Grilled Stuffed Flank Steak Medallions
- U.P. Copper Country Pasties
- Two Way Satay
- Individual Wellington Mignons with Port Wine Sauce
- Grilled Dijon-Apricot Pork Medallions with Apricot Brandy Sauce
- Rum Marinated Grilled Pork Chops with Sweet and Sour Papaya Sauce
- Pork and Apple Pie
- Crusted Lamb Loaf with Tomato-Lemon Sauce
- Mock Muffuletta

- Mango-Wasabi Tuna Steaks
- Mahi-Mahi Caribbean
- Horseradish-Mustard-Mushroom-Sauced Baked Tilapia
- Stuffed Flounder in Puff Pastry
- Smoked Salmon Egg Salad
- Ginger-Curried Tuna Salad
- Greek Feta Shrimp
- Grilled Orange-Coconut Shrimp
- Coconut Crab Cakes
- Shrimp Manicotti
- Thai Red Curry Shrimp Enchiladas
- Scallop, Shrimp, and Artichoke Gratin

- Penne Pastitsio
- Tomato-Basil Tortellini
- Artichoke-Pesto Ravioli Lasagna
- Mushroom-Chicken Garlic-Alfredo Lasagna

- Savory Brunch Cakes
- TBBC Gratin
- Baked Vegetable Frittata
- Mushroom-Bacon-Tomato Pie
- Sausage Golf Balls
- Sticky Rolls

Chicken Strudels

Working with phyllo (or fillo) may at first seem an awkward, labor-intensive task. But it actually is a lot of fun and you'll be rewarded with impressive strudels that go from freezer to oven to table in only 20 minutes.

....

1 pound boneless, skinless chicken breast, cut into 1-inch pieces

¼ cup plus 1 tablespoon canola oil, divided

1 cup chopped red onion

1½ teaspoons grated gingerroot or gingerroot paste

⅓ cup chopped red bell pepper

1 teaspoon lemon sea salt flakes or 1 teaspoon fresh lemon juice and 1 teaspoon salt

¼ teaspoon crushed red pepper flakes

1 teaspoon sesame oil

1 tablespoon soy sauce

1 tablespoon sesame seeds

1 cup finely shredded mozzarella cheese

½ (16-ounce) package phyllo dough, defrosted (about 20 sheets)

Peanut-Coconut Sauce (recipe, page 130), Plum-Ginger Sauce (recipe, page 132), or Sweet and Sour Papaya Sauce (recipe, page 136)

....

At least 1 day or up to 1 month ahead: Place chicken in a food processor and pulse until coarsely chopped. Place 1 tablespoon oil in a large nonstick skillet over medium heat. When oil is hot, add onions and sauté for 2 minutes, until they are soft. Add chicken, gingerroot, bell pepper, lemon salt, and red pepper flakes. Stir to combine. Sauté for 3 minutes, stirring constantly. Add sesame oil and soy sauce and sauté, stirring constantly, until chicken is opaque and no longer pink, about 1 minute more.

Drain chicken mixture in a colander. Return chicken to skillet, off heat. Toss chicken mixture with sesame seeds.

Unroll phyllo dough. Cover with a slightly damp kitchen towel. (Keep towel over phyllo while you are assembling the strudels so phyllo doesn't dry out.) Place a sheet of parchment paper on the kitchen counter. Carefully place 1 sheet phyllo on parchment paper. Brush phyllo gently with canola oil. Place a second sheet of phyllo atop the first. Gently brush sheet with oil. Place ½ cup chicken mixture in a log on the short end of the phyllo, leaving a 1½-inch border of phyllo. Fold sides inward, over the mixture, then roll the phyllo into a cigar-shaped tube. Place a piece of waxed paper in a large, shallow covered container. Place strudel in container, seam side down.

....

Repeat procedure 7 more times. Place a piece of waxed paper atop strudel if a second layer is necessary for storage. Cover container and freeze strudels until needed.

To serve: Preheat oven to 425°F. Place a sheet of aluminum foil on a baking sheet. Coat lightly with vegetable cooking spray. Place frozen strudels on foil, seam-side down. Brush or spray gently with canola oil. Bake for 20 minutes. Remove from oven and allow strudels to cool for 5 minutes. Cut strudels in half on the diagonal with a small, serrated knife. Place 4 strudel halves in a star shape on each of 4 dinner plates. Serve with selected sauce on the side.

Lemon sea salt imparts a unique citrus flavor and is marketed under the brand Bellamessa. Check the website www.opal-export.com for availability.

You'll have a few extra sheets of phyllo left over. For each 2 sheets you have left over, scramble an egg, seasoned with your choice of herbs. Mix with crumbled bacon and shredded Swiss or cheddar cheese. Place ½ cup egg mixture atop phyllo and fold up phyllo as instructed for the chicken strudels. Freeze egg strudels until needed and bake as instructed above. Serve 1 egg strudel per person.

Serves: 4 (2 strudels each)

Chicken Tikka Kabobs

A dish originating in South Asia, chicken tikka is traditionally baked in a clay oven called a tandoor. Marinated in yogurt, herbs, and spices, just as in the original, this version is cooked on a medium-hot grill.

....

3 pounds boneless, skinless chicken breasts, cut into 1½-inch chunks
¼ cup fresh lemon juice
½ teaspoon salt
½ cup nonfat plain yogurt
3 teaspoons minced garlic
1 teaspoon freshly ground coriander seeds
1 teaspoon cumin
1 tablespoon dried sabzitorshi herbs (see "Tips" below)
½ teaspoon gingerroot paste or minced gingerroot
Pinch crushed red pepper flakes
1 large sweet onion, cut into 1½-inch chunks
2 red or yellow bell peppers, seeded and cut into 1½-inch chunks
Pineapple Salsa (recipe, page 131)

....

One day ahead: Place chicken, lemon juice, and salt in a glass or plastic bowl. Stir to combine. Cover and refrigerate for 30 minutes.

Place yogurt, garlic, coriander, cumin, sabzitorshi herbs, gingerroot, and red pepper flakes in a medium bowl and stir to mix well. Add chicken mixture and toss to combine. Transfer to a covered container and refrigerate overnight.

To serve: Heat gas grill to medium-high temperature. Coat 8 metal skewers with vegetable cooking spray. Thread chicken, onions, and peppers on skewers, alternating them, forming 8 kabobs. Grill, turning frequently, for 10 to 15 minutes or until chicken just loses its pink color and becomes opaque. (Do not overcook; chicken will continue cooking after it is removed from the grill.) Serve 2 kabobs per person accompanied with Pineapple Salsa.

....

If you don't have access to a Middle Eastern market to purchase the dried sabzitorshi herbs, you can make your own. Mix equal parts of dried tarragon, savory, basil, parsley, dill, leek, mint, and cilantro. Store herb blend in a zipper bag or glass jar.

Serves: 4

....

Béarnaise Chicken and Biscuit Pie

Farmhouse cookin' at its best, this classic pie is made all the easier by using dried sauce mix and refrigerator biscuits.

3 strips center-cut bacon, cut into small dice

1 cup chopped sweet onions, like Vidalia

8 ounces baby bella mushrooms, wiped clean and thinly sliced

5 ounces baby spinach

1 teaspoon olive oil

1¾ pounds boneless, skinless chicken breasts, cut into bite-size pieces

1 teaspoon garlic paste or finely minced garlic

½ teaspoon lemon-herb seasoning

4 tablespoons butter

1 cup milk

1 (0.9-ounce) package McCormick Béarnaise Sauce Mix

¾ cup shredded cheddar cheese

1 (16.3-ounce) can Pillsbury Grands! Butter Tastin' Biscuits

Early in the day or up to 1 month ahead: Place bacon, onions, and mushrooms in a large nonstick skillet over medium heat. Sauté, stirring frequently, until onions are soft, bacon is crispy, and liquid released from mushrooms has evaporated. Transfer mixture to a large bowl with a slotted spoon. Add spinach to skillet. Sauté, stirring constantly, until spinach has wilted and released water has evaporated. Transfer to bowl.

Place olive oil in skillet. Add chicken and sauté, stirring frequently, for 2 minutes. Add garlic and lemon-herb seasoning and sauté 1 minute more, until chicken has browned. Transfer chicken to bowl. Toss ingredients in bowl to combine well.

Melt butter in a small nonstick saucepan over medium heat. Whisk in milk and sauce mix. Bring to a boil, then reduce heat to low and cook for 1 minute, whisking constantly, until thickened. Pour sauce over chicken mixture. Toss ingredients with sauce until well coated.

Coat a 10-inch deep-dish pie plate with vegetable cooking spray. Transfer chicken mixture to pie plate. Cover with plastic wrap and aluminum foil and refrigerate or freeze until needed.

To serve: Preheat oven to 350°F. Remove plastic wrap and aluminum foil from chicken pie and bring it to room temperature. (Defrost to room temperature if frozen). Re-cover pie with aluminum foil. Bake for 30 minutes. Remove aluminum foil. Sprinkle cheddar cheese over chicken mixture. Place the 8 dough biscuits atop chicken pie and bake for 17 to 19 minutes, until biscuits are golden. Serve immediately.

If you're not fond of tarragon, substitute McCormick Four-Cheese or Creamy Alfredo sauce mixes instead of the béarnaise.

Serves: 4 to 6

Chicken-Vegetable Parmesan

Although this freeze-ahead recipe takes more than an hour to prepare, it makes enough for an army. Assemble in two large baking dishes to serve eight each, or freeze in four 8x8-inch aluminum baking dishes that each will serve four.

....

2 pounds firm eggplant, cut into ½-inch slices (about 2 medium)

1 teaspoon coarse salt

Table salt and freshly ground black pepper

1 pound plum tomatoes, thinly sliced

6 tablespoons olive oil, divided

1 teaspoon garlic paste or finely minced garlic

10 ounces baby bella or button mushrooms, thinly sliced

1 cup grated carrots

15 ounces baby spinach

4 pounds boneless skinless chicken breasts, pounded with a mallet until ¾ inch thick

2 eggs beaten with 2 tablespoons water

1½ cups dried Italian bread crumbs

1 (24-ounce) jar Classico Spicy Tomato & Basil Pasta Sauce

1 (24-ounce) jar Classico Sweet Basil Marinara Sauce

1 pound mozzarella cheese, thinly sliced

1 cup grated Parmesan cheese

....

At least 1 day or up to 1 month ahead: Preheat oven to 350°F. Sprinkle eggplant slices with coarse salt. Place in a colander for 30 minutes. Rinse eggplant slices and pat dry with paper towels. Coat both sides of eggplant slices with olive oil spray. Season to taste with freshly ground black pepper. Place eggplant slices on 2 nonstick baking sheets. Bake for 15 minutes. Turn slices over and bake for 15 minutes more. Remove eggplant from oven and let cool.

Place sliced tomatoes on a nonstick baking sheet. Season with salt and pepper to taste. Bake for 15 minutes. Remove from oven and let cool.

Meanwhile, place 1 tablespoon olive oil in a large nonstick skillet over medium heat. Add garlic, mushrooms, carrots, and ¼ teaspoon salt. Sauté, stirring frequently, for 5 minutes or until released liquid has evaporated. Transfer to a dinner plate and set aside.

Heat 1 tablespoon oil in a large nonstick skillet over medium heat. Add half the spinach and sauté, stirring constantly, until spinach has wilted and released moisture has evaporated. Repeat with remaining spinach. Transfer to a dinner plate and set aside.

....

Cut pounded chicken breasts into serving-size pieces. (You should have 16 pieces.) Place egg wash in a shallow dish. Place bread crumbs on a dinner plate. Dip each chicken breast into egg wash. Then press both sides into bread crumbs. Place on a large tray or baking sheet.

Sauté chicken in 3 batches. Place 1 tablespoon oil in a large nonstick skillet over medium heat. Sauté for 2 minutes per side, until chicken is lightly browned. Remove from skillet and place on a large plate. Repeat process with remaining 2 tablespoons oil and 2 batches of chicken breasts.

To assemble: Coat two 9x13-inch baking dishes with olive oil spray. Mix pasta sauces together in a large bowl. In each dish, layer ingredients, beginning with 1 cup sauce on the bottom of dish. Place half the eggplant slices in a layer atop sauce. Spread half the carrot-mushroom mixture over eggplant. Spread half the spinach over carrot-mushroom mixture. Season with salt and freshly ground black pepper to taste. Place half the chicken breasts atop spinach (8 per dish). Spread 1½ cups sauce over chicken. Place a layer of mozzarella on sauce. Place half the tomato slices atop mozzarella. Sprinkle ½ cup Parmesan cheese over tomatoes.

Cover each dish with plastic wrap and then aluminum foil. Refrigerate for 24 hours or freeze until needed.

To serve: Bring Chicken-Vegetable Parmesan to room temperature. Preheat oven to 350°F. Bake, uncovered, for 45 minutes or until all ingredients have heated through and mixture is bubbly.

Pounding the chicken breasts makes them a more uniform size. Boneless chicken breasts come in all sizes, so cut the very large ones into serving-size pieces after pounding.

Serves: 16

Cranberry–Pistachio Stuffed Chicken Breast Salad

This is a great luncheon dish or a showy, colorful offering at a picnic or tailgate party. It is equally delicious served at room temperature or straight from the oven.

½ cup dried cranberries

¼ cup sugar

⅓ cup merlot wine

1 cup sour cream

1 tablespoon Dijon mustard

2½ tablespoons honey

¼ cup chopped shelled, roasted, salted pistachio nuts

4 plump boneless, skinless chicken breasts

2 tablespoons olive oil

½ teaspoon lemon-herb seasoning

3 cups baby greens

Early in the day or 1 day ahead: Place cranberries, sugar, and wine in a small bowl. Stir to mix well. Cover with plastic wrap and set aside at room temperature for 1 hour.

Meanwhile, mix together sour cream, mustard, and honey in a medium bowl. Cover with plastic wrap and refrigerate until needed.

Preheat oven to 350°F. Drain cranberry mixture in a strainer. Return cranberries to bowl and add pistachios. Stir to mix well.

With a sharp knife, slice each chicken breast horizontally, stopping about ¾ inch from the edge, forming a flapped pocket. Lift the flap and place one-quarter of the cranberry-pistachio mixture on the chicken breast. Pull the flap securely over the stuffing mixture. Transfer each breast to an 11x7-inch baking dish that has been coated with vegetable cooking spray.

Brush chicken breasts with olive oil and sprinkle each with lemon-herb seasoning. Bake for 25 to 30 minutes, until just barely pink when tested with a knife. Remove from oven (chicken will continue to cook) and allow chicken breasts to cool. Transfer to a covered container and refrigerate until needed.

To serve: Allow chicken breasts to reach room temperature. Place ¾ cup baby greens on each of 4 dinner plates. Slice each chicken breast crosswise into ½-inch pieces, taking care to keep stuffing in place. Place slices in a fan shape atop greens. Drizzle a rope of honey-Dijon sour cream sauce onto the fan of chicken slices.

You can also assemble stuffed chicken breasts early in the day and refrigerate them, uncooked, in a covered container until needed for dinner. Bake as instructed above and serve warm with honey-Dijon sour cream sauce drizzled on top. Serve with Fruited Chutney Rice (recipe, page 108).

Serves: 4

Chicken Saltimbocca Roulades

The Italian word "saltimbocca" means "jumps into the mouth," and it is clear that the flavorful combination of proscuitto, mozzarella, and sage makes these chicks a lively taste sensation. Made ahead and frozen until needed, this is a perfect no-fuss dinner party recipe.

4 boneless, skinless chicken breasts (about 2 pounds)

4 thin slices prosciutto

4 (1-ounce) slices fresh mozzarella cheese, slivered

1 teaspoon dried sage, divided

4 tablespoons butter, melted, plus 1 teaspoon at room temperature

½ cup Italian bread crumbs

3 tablespoons grated Parmesan cheese

3 tablespoons snipped fresh flat-leaf parsley

Tomato-Caper Hollandaise Sauce (recipe, page 137)

Early in the day or up to 2 weeks ahead: Place each chicken breast between 2 large pieces of waxed paper and pound with a mallet until they are about ⅓ inch thick. Top each pounded chicken breast with 1 slice prosciutto and one-quarter of the slivered mozzarella. Sprinkle each with ¼ teaspoon sage.

Roll up each chicken breast, securing rolls with a sturdy wooden toothpick. Skewer each roll end with a toothpick, making sure ham and cheese are tucked inside.

Grease a 7x11-inch baking dish with 1 teaspoon butter. Mix bread crumbs, Parmesan cheese, and parsley together on a dinner plate. Place melted butter in a shallow bowl. Dip each rolled chicken breast in butter, coating all sides. Roll breasts in bread crumb mixture, making sure all sides are well coated with crumbs. Place each crumb-coated roll, seam down, in buttered baking dish. Cover dish with plastic wrap and refrigerate until needed. (If freezing chicken roulades, transfer them to a covered container and freeze until needed. Defrost to room temperature before proceeding with recipe.)

To serve: Preheat oven to 350°F. Remove plastic wrap and bake roulades for 40 to 45 minutes, until chicken is just cooked through and no longer pink when cut with a sharp knife. Place one roulade on each dinner plate. Remove toothpicks. Cut each roulade into ½-inch slices and fan them on plate. Top with Tomato-Caper Hollandaise Sauce. Serve immediately.

Saltimbocca is traditionally made with veal, but it is just as wonderful with chicken. You can substitute veal in this recipe, but cut the baking time in half.

Serves: 4

Tomato-Coconut Chicken Curry

This sweet and spicy Indian-style curry tastes best when served with coconut-infused rice. Simply substitute coconut milk for half the required water in whatever rice recipe you are following.

1 tablespoon olive oil

3 cups thinly sliced sweet onions, like Vidalia

1 teaspoon garlic paste or finely minced garlic

½ tablespoon gingerroot paste or finely minced gingerroot

1 jalapeño pepper, seeded and minced (about 1 tablespoon)

1½ tablespoons mild curry powder

3 (14.5-ounce) cans unseasoned petite diced tomatoes, drained

2 teaspoons sugar

1 teaspoon salt

½ teaspoon crushed red pepper flakes

1 tablespoon fresh lemon juice

1 (14-ounce) can coconut milk

2 pounds boneless, skinless chicken breasts, thinly sliced

¼ cup snipped fresh basil

½ cup sweetened coconut, toasted

One day ahead: Place olive oil in an extra-large nonstick skillet over medium heat. Add onions, garlic, gingerroot, and jalapeños and sauté, stirring constantly, for 2 minutes. Add curry powder and sauté for 1 minute more, stirring constantly. Add tomatoes, sugar, salt, red pepper flakes, and lemon juice. Stir to combine. Reduce heat to low. Add coconut milk and cook for 3 minutes, stirring frequently.

Add chicken to sauce mixture. Cook for 10 minutes, stirring frequently, until chicken has almost cooked through. (Don't overcook chicken; it will continue to cook when you reheat the curry before serving.) Remove from heat and stir in the basil. Transfer to a covered container and refrigerate until needed.

To serve: Place chicken curry in an extra-large nonstick skillet over low heat. Cook gently, just until sauce and chicken have heated through, 10 to 15 minutes. Transfer to a large shallow serving bowl. Sprinkle curry with toasted coconut and serve immediately.

Sharwood's or Madras curry powders are good mild brands to use in this recipe. You can easily slice the chicken breasts thinly if you freeze them slightly first. Freeze jalapeños whole when you find them plentiful in season. To use, dip frozen jalapeño in warm water, then cut it in half lengthwise and scoop out seeds with a small spoon before mincing.

Serves: 6

Turkey Picadillo

Pronounced 'pick-a-DEE-yo,' this revamped classic Cuban dish is usually made with ground beef. Like the original, this lighter version tastes best when made in advance, for as in any good relationship, its unique flavors marry and mellow with time.

1 tablespoon olive oil

½ cup chopped sweet onions, like Vidalia

½ cup chopped red bell peppers

2 teaspoons garlic paste or finely minced garlic

1 pound ground turkey

½ teaspoon ground cumin

½ teaspoon salt

¼ teaspoon black pepper

3 tablespoons tomato paste with basil, garlic, and oregano

½ cup raisins

¼ cup finely chopped pimento-stuffed green olives

1 tablespoon capers, rinsed and drained

½ teaspoon olive juice

½ cup chardonnay or other dry white wine

Three days or up to 1 month ahead: Warm oil in a large nonstick skillet over medium heat. Add onions, bell peppers, and garlic, and cook, stirring frequently, until onions have softened, about 2 minutes.

Meanwhile, place ground turkey in a medium bowl and add cumin, salt, and pepper. Mix seasonings into turkey with clean hands. Add turkey to the skillet and cook, stirring frequently, for 3 minutes, until turkey has just lost its pink color and becomes opaque. Reduce heat to low. Add tomato paste, raisins, olives, capers, and olive juice. Stir to combine. Cook for 2 minutes, stirring frequently. Stir in wine and continue cooking for 1 minute more.

Remove picadillo from burner and transfer to a covered container. Refrigerate, uncovered, for 10 minutes so that picadillo can cool. Cover container and refrigerate or freeze until needed.

To serve: Defrost picadillo, if frozen. Reheat picadillo gently in a large nonstick skillet over low heat.

Classically picadillo is served with rice and fried plantains, but this dish is very versatile. Try making moyettes, sort of a Cuban Sloppy Joe: Cut the top off a 3-inch roll. Hollow out the bread crumbs. Toast top and hollowed-out roll in the oven for a couple of minutes. Fill with picadillo and replace top-hat crust. Or, mix picadillo with hot penne pasta or steamed spaghetti squash. Picadillo also makes a great filling for soft tacos or enchiladas or a meat base for nachos.

Serves: 4

47

Pizza Potpie

In 2 B.C., French bakers encased a lamprey in pastry and gave it to their king, a delicacy he very much enjoyed. So this Pizza Potpie is not the first pie in history to hold a surprise under the crust! Using turkey sausage and part-skim cheeses reduces the fat content and greasiness of this savory dish — not to mention the guilt — and no flavor is lost in the transition. This is a great dish to keep on hand in the freezer.

1 (19½-ounce) package Italian sweet turkey sausage

1 (19½-ounce) package Italian hot turkey sausage

1 (25-ounce) jar spicy marinara sauce

1½ cups part-skim ricotta cheese

⅓ cup grated Parmesan cheese

⅓ cup snipped fresh flat leaf parsley

1 teaspoon dried oregano

1 teaspoon dried marjoram

1 teaspoon dried basil

2 eggs, divided

Freshly ground black pepper

1 (8-ounce) package shredded part-skim mozzarella cheese (2½ cups)

1 (10-ounce) cylinder Pillsbury Pizza Crust

1 tablespoon water

Two days or up to 1 month ahead: Remove casings from sausages and crumble meat. Sauté crumbled sausage in a large nonstick skillet over medium heat until cooked through and browned, about 10 minutes. Drain well in a sieve and transfer sausage to a large bowl. Add spicy marinara sauce to sausage and mix well to combine. Set aside.

Place ricotta and Parmesan cheeses, parsley, oregano, marjoram, and basil in a medium bowl. Stir to mix. Place 1 egg in a small bowl and beat it lightly with a fork. Add egg to cheese mixture and stir to combine. Add pepper to taste. Set aside.

Coat a 10-inch deep-dish pie plate with vegetable cooking spray. Place half the sausage mixture evenly in bottom of pie plate. Dot half the cheese and egg mixture evenly over sausage mixture. Top with half the mozzarella cheese. Repeat layers with remaining ingredients.

Cover pizza potpie with plastic wrap and aluminum foil and refrigerate for up to 2 days or freeze for up to a month. (Defrost thoroughly before baking.)

To serve: Preheat oven to 350°F. Remove plastic wrap and foil from pie plate. Unroll pizza dough onto a large sheet of parchment paper and stretch it into a circle about 1-inch larger than the deep-dish pie plate. Transfer pizza dough to top of pizza pie, smoothing dough evenly and tucking excess dough inside the dish around sausage mixture. Place 1 egg and 1 tablespoon water in a small bowl and beat together with a fork. Brush egg wash evenly over pizza crust. Bake for 40 to 45 minutes, or until top is golden brown. Remove potpie from oven and allow it to rest for 10 minutes before serving.

. . . .

I use Emeril's Kicked Up Tomato Pasta Sauce in this recipe because I think it adds an extra-special zing, but any spicy marinara sauce will work.

Serves: 8
. . . .

Meatballs Four Ways

Make today meatball day! Mix up a batch of meatball base, divide it into four portions, spice each portion differently, roll and bake meatballs, then freeze them in freezer-weight zipper bags. Use the meatballs to create four distinctly different dishes: Greek Meatballs with Mediterranean Penne, Thai Meatballs in Red Curry Sauce with Jasmine Rice, Hawaiian Meatballs in Sweet and Sour Sauce with Coconut Rice, and Sicilian Meatballs in Fresh Tomato Sauce with Spaghetti (recipes on following pages).

MEATBALL BASE

1 pound ground lamb

1 pound ground pork

2½ pounds ground beef (chuck)

2 cups chopped sweet onions, like Vidalia

2 cups dried Japanese panko bread crumbs

2 teaspoons salt

½ teaspoon black pepper

4 large eggs

½ cup milk

2 teaspoons garlic paste or minced garlic

Up to 2 months ahead: Place lamb, pork, and ground beef in a large bowl. Add onions, bread crumbs, salt, and pepper. Using clean hands, mix ingredients together until well combined.

Place eggs, milk, and garlic in a small bowl. Whisk together until blended. Pour egg mixture atop meat mixture. Mix ingredients together well with clean hands.

Divide meatball mixture equally among 4 medium bowls (about 1 pound 7 ounces per bowl). Season meatball mixture in each bowl using the 4 recipes that follow.

HAWAIIAN MEATBALLS

½ cup chopped water chestnuts

1 tablespoon soy sauce

2 teaspoons sesame oil

1 teaspoon gingerroot paste or minced gingerroot

½ teaspoon crushed red pepper flakes

¼ cup chopped sliced almonds

¼ of the meatball base mixture

Add water chestnuts, soy sauce, sesame oil, gingerroot, red pepper flakes, and almonds to meatball base mixture. Mix ingredients together well with clean hands.

THAI MEATBALLS

1 tablespoon grated orange zest
1 tablespoon Asian sweet chili sauce
1 teaspoon fish sauce

1 teaspoon gingerroot paste
  or minced gingerroot
2 tablespoons snipped fresh mint
¼ of the meatball base mixture

Add orange zest, chili sauce, fish sauce, gingerroot, and mint to meatball base mixture. Mix ingredients together well with clean hands.

GREEK MEATBALLS

½ cup crumbled feta cheese
¼ cup chopped, seeded kalamata olives
¼ cup chopped roasted red bell peppers

2 teaspoons grated lemon zest
1 teaspoon Greek seasoning, like Penzeys
¼ of the meatball base mixture

Add cheese, olives, roasted peppers, lemon zest, and Greek seasoning to meatball base mixture. Mix ingredients together well with clean hands.

SICILIAN MEATBALLS

3 tablespoons snipped fresh flat-leaf parsley
1½ teaspoon Italian seasoning, like Penzeys
½ cup grated Parmesan cheese

¼ cup dry-toasted pine nuts
¼ cup dried currants
¼ of the meatball base mixture

Add parsley, Italian seasoning, Parmesan cheese, pine nuts, and currants to meatball base mixture. Mix ingredients together well with clean hands.

To make meatballs: Preheat oven to 400°F. Working with one type of meatball at a time, form meatball mixture into 2-inch balls. Place each in the cup of a mini muffin pan. Bake for 15 minutes. Turn meatballs over in muffin cups and bake for 8 minutes longer. Repeat process until all meatballs have been baked. Remove meatballs from muffin cups and place each type on a separate dinner plate to cool.

To store meatballs: Place cooled meatballs in freezer-weight zipper bags by variety. Label and freeze until needed.

To serve meatballs: Use meatballs in the 4 recipes that follow.

The baking process moves along faster if you have several 18-count mini muffin pans.

Makes: 18 meatballs of each variety (72 meatballs total)

Greek Meatballs with Mediterranean-Sauced Penne

Kalamata olives, capers, tomatoes, and feta cheese marry in this no-cook sauce that goes together in minutes.

2½ cups chopped fresh plum tomatoes (about 1 pound)

3 tablespoons minced, seeded kalamata olives

1 tablespoon capers, rinsed and drained

1 teaspoon garlic paste or minced garlic

¼ teaspoon salt

⅛ teaspoon crushed red pepper flakes

1 tablespoon red wine vinegar

1 tablespoon olive oil

2 tablespoons snipped fresh basil

½ pound penne pasta

18 frozen Greek meatballs, defrosted (recipe, page 51)

1 cup beef broth

½ cup crumbled tomato-basil feta cheese, divided

Early in the day, make Mediterranean Sauce: Combine tomatoes, olives, capers, garlic, salt, crushed red pepper flakes, vinegar, olive oil, and basil in a medium bowl. Toss to mix well. Transfer to a covered container and refrigerate until needed.

To serve: Bring a large pot water to boil over high heat. Add penne. Reduce heat to medium and cook to al dente, about 12 minutes, following package instructions.

Meanwhile, remove Mediterranean Sauce from refrigerator and place it in a large serving bowl. Allow sauce to come to room temperature. Place meatballs and beef broth in a large nonstick skillet over medium-low heat. Simmer for 10 minutes, until meatballs are heated through.

Drain penne and toss it with Mediterranean Sauce. Add ¼ cup feta cheese and toss to combine. Remove meatballs from broth with a slotted spoon and place in a serving bowl. Sprinkle remaining feta cheese over meatballs. Serve sauced penne and meatballs immediately.

Kalamata olives are oil-cured black olives often used in Mediterranean dishes. You can find them with conventional olives in your supermarket.

Serves: 4

Thai Meatballs in Red Curry Sauce with Jasmine Rice

Defrosting the meatballs in the Red Curry Sauce adds a little bit of water to the sauce, which thins it nicely upon reheating.

1 (14-ounce) can coconut milk

2 teaspoons red curry paste

2 tablespoons brown sugar

1 tablespoon fish sauce

1 tablespoon fresh lime juice

⅓ cup snipped fresh basil

1½ cups jasmine rice

18 frozen Thai meatballs (recipe, page 51)

Early in the day or the day before, make Red Curry Sauce: Heat coconut milk in a large nonstick saucepan over medium-low heat. Add red curry paste and stir until melted. Add brown sugar, fish sauce, and lime juice and stir until sugar is melted. Stir in basil. Simmer for 1 minute. Add frozen meatballs to curry sauce. Stir to combine. Transfer meatballs and sauce to a covered container and refrigerate until needed.

To serve: Bring 3 cups water to a boil in a medium saucepan over medium heat. Stir in rice. Cover saucepan, reduce heat to low, and simmer until water is absorbed, about 15 to 20 minutes. Fluff rice with a fork.

While rice is cooking, place meatballs and red curry sauce in a large nonstick saucepan over low heat. Simmer for 10 minutes, stirring gently and turning meatballs, until meatballs and sauce are heated through. Serve atop hot jasmine rice.

 You'll find jasmine rice in the international section of your supermarket.

Serves: 4 to 6

Hawaiian Meatballs in Sweet and Sour Sauce with Coconut Rice

This Sweet and Sour Sauce reflects the multiple culinary cultures fused in the flavors of Hawaii.

....

1 tablespoon olive oil

1 teaspoon garlic paste or finely minced garlic

1 teaspoon gingerroot paste or finely minced gingerroot

1 cup finely chopped onions

1 cup chopped red bell pepper

1 cup chopped green bell pepper

2 (8-ounce) cans pineapple chunks in own juice

2 cups chicken broth

3 tablespoons soy sauce

¼ cup cider vinegar

3 tablespoons brown sugar

2 tablespoons honey

½ teaspoon Chinese Five Spice seasoning

18 frozen Hawaiian meatballs (recipe, page 50)

1½ cups basmati rice

1 cup coconut milk

2 tablespoons cornstarch

¼ cup sweetened flaked coconut, dry-toasted

¼ cup sliced almonds, dry-toasted

....

Up to 1 month ahead, make the Sweet and Sour Sauce: Place olive oil in a large nonstick skillet over medium heat. When oil is hot add garlic, gingerroot, and onions. Sauté for 1 minute, stirring constantly. Add bell peppers and sauté for 1 minute. Transfer mixture to a dinner plate.

Drain juice from pineapple chunks in a sieve, reserving juice. Cut each pineapple chunk in half and set aside. Place juice in skillet. Add broth, soy sauce, vinegar, brown sugar, honey, and five spice seasoning. Stir ingredients, increase heat to medium-high, and bring mixture to a boil. Reduce heat to low and simmer, uncovered, for 5 minutes.

Remove skillet from stove. Add onion mixture and pineapple chunks. Transfer to a covered

....

container and place in refrigerator, uncovered, to cool. When sauce is cool, cover container and freeze until needed.

Early in the day: Defrost meatballs and sauce.

To serve: Wash rice until water runs clear. Drain in a colander. Place coconut milk and 2 cups water in a medium saucepan over medium heat. Bring mixture to a boil and stir in rice. Place 3 pieces of paper toweling atop rim of pan. Place cover tightly on pan, reduce heat to low, and simmer rice for 20 minutes, until liquid has been absorbed, Fluff rice with a fork before serving.

Meanwhile, place sauce in a large nonstick saucepan over medium-low heat. Mix 2 tablespoons cornstarch with 2 tablespoons sauce liquid. Stir cornstarch mixture into sauce. Add meatballs to sauce. Simmer on low heat for 15 minutes, until meatballs have heated through and sauce has thickened. (If sauce is too thin, mix 1 more tablespoon cornstarch with 1 tablespoon warm sauce liquid, stir into sauce, and simmer for several more minutes.) Place meatballs and sauce in a large shallow serving bowl. Mix coconut and almonds together in a small bowl. Serve meatballs and sauce atop coconut rice. Sprinkle coconut-almond mixture over each serving.

....

The best place to buy basmati rice is at a wholesale club like Sam's Club, BJ's or Costco. You'll find the rice packaged in 5 pound burlap bags. It will keep indefinitely in the pantry.

Serves: 4 to 6
....

Sicilian Meatballs in Fresh Tomato Sauce with Spaghetti

Even the godfather would love these classically Italian meatballs, which bask in a smooth, garlicky sauce made from fresh plum tomatoes.

2 tablespoons olive oil

1½ cups chopped sweet onions, like Vidalia

2 teaspoons minced garlic or garlic paste

5 cups (about 3 pounds) ripe plum tomatoes, peeled, seeded, and diced

1 teaspoon dried marjoram

2 teaspoons dried basil

1½ teaspoons salt

1 pound dried spaghetti

18 frozen Sicilian meatballs (recipe, page 51)

Up to I month ahead, make Fresh Tomato Sauce: Heat olive oil in a large nonstick saucepan over medium heat. Add onions and sauté, stirring frequently, for 3 minutes. Add garlic and sauté, stirring frequently, for 1 minute more. Add tomatoes and stir to mix well with onions. Cook tomato mixture for 15 minutes, stirring frequently.

Transfer tomato mixture to a blender and pulse until tomatoes are pureed. Wipe out saucepan and return tomato mixture to pan. Add marjoram, basil, and salt. Reduce heat to low, place saucepan on stove, and simmer, stirring frequently, for 10 minutes.

Transfer tomato sauce to a covered container. Place in refrigerator, uncovered, for 30 minutes, so that sauce can quickly cool. Cover container and refrigerate until needed (up to 3 days) or freeze (up to 1 month).

Early in the day: Defrost meatballs and tomato sauce.

To serve: Bring a large pot of water to boil. Add spaghetti to pot and cook to al dente, following package instructions, about 10 to 12 minutes.

Meanwhile, place meatballs and sauce in a large saucepan over medium-low heat. Reheat, stirring gently, until both are heated through, about 10 to 15 minutes. Place in a large serving bowl. Toss with spaghetti and serve immediately.

 This sauce is a great base for pizza as well. Top pizza with leftover meatballs.

Serves: 4 to 6

Duck Breasts with Raspberry Port Sauce

Elegant and guilt-free, these boneless, skinless duck breasts bathe in a pool of ruby port sauce. Definitely company fare!

2 tablespoons butter, divided

1 shallot, minced

¼ cup port wine

¼ cup white wine

3 tablespoons seedless raspberry preserves

1 tablespoon balsamic vinegar

1 tablespoon Dijon mustard

1 cup fresh or frozen raspberries plus a few for garnish

4 boneless duck breasts, skin-on

Salt and freshly ground black pepper

Up to 2 days ahead: Make Raspberry Port Sauce. Place 1 tablespoon butter in a small saucepan over medium-low heat. When butter has melted, add shallots and sauté, stirring frequently, until they are soft and translucent, about 2 minutes. Add wines and bring to a boil. Cook for 6 minutes, stirring frequently, until mixture has reduced to 3 tablespoons.

Reduce heat to low and add preserves, vinegar, and mustard. Cook, stirring constantly, until mixture is smooth, about 1 minute. Add 1 cup raspberries and cook, stirring frequently, until raspberries have broken up and mixture is smooth, about 3 minutes. Add 1 tablespoon butter to sauce and stir until it is melted. Remove sauce from heat and transfer it to a container. Refrigerate, uncovered, until cooled. Cover container and refrigerate until needed.

Up to 6 hours ahead: Place a large nonstick skillet over medium-high heat. Add duck breasts, skin-side down. Partially cover skillet so grease will not splatter and cook for 5 minutes. Turn breasts over and cook them for 2 minutes more. Transfer duck breasts to a plate and allow them to cool. Remove skin from cooled duck breasts and discard. Place breasts in a shallow baking pan that has been coated with vegetable cooking spray. Cover with aluminum foil and refrigerate until needed.

Twenty minutes before serving: Preheat oven to 450°F. Remove duck breasts from refrigerator and bring to room temperature, about 5 minutes. Place Raspberry Port Sauce in a small saucepan over low heat and heat until it is warmed through, stirring occasionally.

Season duck breasts with salt and pepper to taste. Roast breasts, uncovered, for 6 to 8 minutes, until they are still slightly pink when tested with a sharp knife. Remove duck breasts from oven and allow them to rest for 5 minutes. (Duck will continue cooking.) Thinly slice breasts on the diagonal.

Place a small pool of Raspberry-Port sauce on each of 4 dinner plates. Place duck slices from each breast in a fan atop sauce on each plate. Garnish with a couple of raspberries.

During berry season, try using a mix of fresh berries in addition to raspberries, such as strawberries, blueberries, or blackberries. You can use other berry flavored preserves as well.

Serves: 4

Mustard and Jack Daniel's Marinated Sirloin Steak

Jack is back in this whiskey-infused steak marinade perfect for a summer cookout. Serve with Twice Baked Stuffed Potatoes (recipe, page 109) and Warm Caprese Salad (recipe, page 102).

½ cup Vidalia onion mustard

¼ cup Jack Daniel's whiskey or bourbon

½ cup plus 2 tablespoons packed dark brown sugar

2 teaspoons Worcestershire sauce

3 pounds sirloin steak, cut 1¼ inches thick

One day ahead: Mix mustard, whiskey, brown sugar, and Worcestershire sauce together in a small bowl. Place steak in a freezer-weight zipper bag. Pour marinade into bag. Close bag and massage bag until steak is totally covered with marinade. Place in refrigerator overnight.

To serve: Preheat grill to medium-hot (450°F). Remove steak from marinade. Place marinade in a microwave-safe container and microwave for 1 minute. Grill steak, basting with marinade and turning once, until medium-rare, about 5 to 6 minutes per side. Remove steak from grill. Cut slices on a slight angle, about ⅜ inch thick. Serve immediately.

Vidalia onion mustard can be found in gourmet-type food stores or can be ordered from on-line markets. Substitute a mixture of ¼ cup finely minced sweet onions and ½ cup Dijon or whole-seed mustard if you can't find the more exotic version.

Serves: 8

Grilled Stuffed Flank Steak Medallions

The ease of preparing this recipe belies the spectacular presentation. (You'll need six 6-inch wooden skiewers to make the steak roll in this recipe.) For a more simple everyday meal, follow marinating instructions, then grill steak and slice it thinly on the diagonal.

⅓ cup soy sauce

⅓ cup red wine vinegar

2 tablespoons honey

2 tablespoons canola oil

2 teaspoons garlic paste or minced garlic

½ teaspoon dry mustard

½ teaspoon gingerroot paste or
    grated, peeled gingerroot

¼ cup cracked pepper

¼ cup chopped sweet onions, like Vidalia

1 pound flank steak

½ cup blue cheese

2 tablespoons heavy cream

⅓ cup julienne-cut sun-dried tomatoes
    (not oil-packed)

¾ cup julienne-cut baby spinach

One day ahead: Whisk together soy sauce, vinegar, honey, canola oil, garlic paste, mustard, gingerroot, pepper, and onions in a small bowl. Set aside.

Place steak on a cutting board and pound both sides with a meat mallet until steak is ¼ to ⅓ inch thick. Place steak in a freezer-weight zipper bag. Pour marinade over steak, massaging steak so that it is totally covered with marinade. Close bag and refrigerate for 24 hours.

Early in the day of grilling: Remove steak from marinade. Discard marinade. Place steak on a cutting board. Mix blue cheese and cream together in a small bowl until smooth. Spread mixture, lengthwise, down the center of the steak, in a 2-inch-wide line. Sprinkle sun-dried tomatoes over cheese. Pack spinach over tomatoes. Starting at one of the long sides, roll steak up tightly over filling, until overlapping edge is on top. Secure steak roll with six 6-inch (or longer) wooden skewers spaced at regular intervals, about 1½ inch apart, pushing each skewer into the overlapping edge and completely through the steak roll. Cover with aluminum foil and refrigerate until needed.

To serve: Preheat grill to medium-hot (about 450°F). Use a large serrated knife to cut steak roll between skewers, forming 6 steak medallions, each about 1½ inches thick. Grill for 3½ minutes per side (medium-rare), carefully turning them with a spatula so that filling doesn't fall out. Serve immediately.

To julienne-cut spinach, stack leaves in a pile and cut across pile with kitchen scissors, forming narrow strips. If you don't like blue cheese, you can use any commercial cheese spread of your choice. Thin cheese with a tablespoon of cream, if necessary, to achieve a spreadable consistency.

Serves: 6

U.P. Copper Country Pasties

Once the lunchtime fare of Michigan's copper miners, pasties are still ubiquitous in the state's Upper Peninsula. Pasty shops in the Michigan towns offer unusual and innovative fillings for the pastry-encased savory pies, but tradition demands a simple filling of ground meat, potatoes, and onions, always eaten topped with ketchup.

1 tablespoon olive oil, divided

1½ cups chopped onions, like Vidalia

3 cups diced (¼-inch) potatoes, like Yukon Gold

1 pound ground beef

1 pound ground pork

Seasoned salt

Freshly ground black pepper

2 (15-ounce) packages rolled Pillsbury pie crusts (2 in each package), at room temperature

1 egg, beaten with 1 tablespoon water

Ketchup

Up to 1 month ahead: Place 2 teaspoons olive oil in a large nonstick skillet over medium heat. When oil is hot, add onions and potatoes and sauté, stirring frequently, until onions are soft, about 2½ minutes. Transfer mixture to a large bowl.

Place remaining 1 teaspoon olive oil in skillet. Add ground beef and cook, stirring frequently, until meat is browned. Transfer beef to bowl with a slotted spoon. Add ground pork to skillet and cook, stirring frequently, until browned. Transfer pork to bowl with a slotted spoon. Sprinkle with seasoned salt and freshly ground black pepper to taste. Set aside.

Place 1 pie crust atop a large piece of parchment paper. Roll dough with a rolling pin until it is large enough to cut out two 7-inch circles of dough. (Use a saucepan lid as your template and cut around the edge with a sharp paring knife.) Place ½ cup meat mixture in the lower half of each circle. Bring other side of dough circle over filling, creating a half-moon. Crimp the edges of the dough into a firm seam. Cut 3 small steam vents in the top of the pasty and place it on a nonstick baking sheet. Repeat this process with remaining 3 pie crusts, reserving cut-away dough. Form cut-away dough into a ball and roll it out, cutting as many 7-inch circles of dough as you can and repeating the filling/crimping process. Place trays of pasties in the freezer until frozen solid. Transfer them to a large covered container. Separate layers with waxed paper. Freeze until needed.

To serve: Preheat oven to 400°F. Defrost pasties to room temperature on a nonstick baking sheet that has been lightly coated with vegetable cooking spray. Brush tops of pasties with egg wash. Bake for 20 to 25 minutes, until crust is golden brown and filling has heated through. Serve with a side of ketchup.

You can use all ground beef in the pasties if you wish. I like to use Penzeys 4S Special Seasoned Salt, but any seasoned salt will work in this recipe.

Makes: 12 pasties (1 to 2 per serving)

Two-Way Satay

Satays are skewered meats similar to kabobs, but the meat is cut into thinner strips. A popular street food in Indonesia, satay is usually accompanied by a special sauce. Serve the beef satay with Peanut-Coconut Sauce and the pork satay with Sweet Garlic Sauce.

½ cup pineapple juice

¼ cup soy sauce

¼ cup chopped scallions, both white and green parts

6 teaspoons sesame seeds, divided

1 packed tablespoon brown sugar

4 teaspoons garlic paste or finely minced garlic, divided

¼ teaspoon black pepper

1 pound pork tenderloin, cut into ¾-inch strips

½ cup coconut milk

⅓ cup fresh lime juice

1 tablespoon minced red chilies with seeds

1 tablespoon chopped lemongrass or 1 tablespoon chopped lemon

1 teaspoon ground coriander

½ teaspoon ground cumin

2 tablespoons fish sauce

1 teaspoon sugar

1 pound beef tenderloin tidbits, cut into ¾-inch strips

Peanut-Coconut Sauce (recipe, page 130)

Sweet Garlic Sauce (recipe, page 135)

At least 24 hours or up to 2 days ahead: Whisk together pineapple juice, soy sauce, scallions, 4 teaspoons sesame seeds, brown sugar, 1 teaspoon garlic paste, and black pepper in a medium bowl. Place pork tenderloin strips in a large freezer-weight zipper bag. Pour marinade over pork. Seal bag and refrigerate.

In a medium bowl, whisk together coconut milk, lime juice, chilies, lemongrass, 3 teaspoons garlic paste, coriander, cumin, fish sauce, and sugar. Place beef strips in a large freezer-weight zipper bag. Pour marinade over beef. Seal bag and refrigerate.

To serve: Preheat gas grill. Remove beef and pork from marinade and thread meat strips onto 8 thin skewers that have been coated with vegetable cooking spray. (You'll have 4 pork and 4 beef skewers.) Sprinkle remaining 2 teaspoons sesame seeds over skewered pork strips. Grill pork skewers for 4 minutes per side, turning once. Grill beef skewers for 2½ minutes per side, turning once. Serve 1 skewer of each meat per person accompanied by both dipping sauces.

If you trim out a whole beef tenderloin to make Individual Wellington Mignons (recipe, page 62), you can use the tidbits from the trimming for the beef satay. Or you can use top sirloin, but be sure to marinate it for 2 days as it is a tougher cut of meat.

Serves: 4

Individual Wellington Mignons with Port Wine Sauce

When the occasion calls for a special dinner entrée with the "wow" factor, this is the dish to serve. Assembly of the Wellingtons is admittedly labor-intensive, but all the prep can be done one day ahead so you need only pop them in the oven for a short time before serving.

2 tablespoons olive oil, divided

8 filet mignon steaks, cut 1½ to 1¾ inches thick

2 tablespoons butter, divided

½ pound baby bella or button mushrooms, finely chopped

1 (8-ounce) carton sun-dried tomato and basil cream cheese spread, softened at room temperature

¼ cup seasoned Italian dry bread crumbs

1 tablespoon snipped fresh chives

¼ teaspoon salt

1 tablespoon port wine

3 tablespoons flour, divided

1½ (17.3-ounce) packages frozen puff pastry sheets (3 sheets), thawed in refrigerator

1 egg, beaten with 1 tablespoon water

Port Wine Sauce, heated (recipe, page 133)

Up to 1 day ahead: Place 1 tablespoon oil in a large nonstick skillet over medium-high heat. When oil is hot, place 4 steaks in skillet. Sear for 3 minutes. (When searing the steaks, grease will splatter out of the pan. Use a splatter guard or hold a skillet cover about 1 inch above skillet.) Turn steaks and sear another minute. Using tongs, transfer steaks to a large plate. Wipe out skillet with paper toweling. Add remaining 1 tablespoon oil to skillet. When oil is hot, place remaining 4 steaks in skillet and sear as instructed above. Refrigerate seared steaks for 30 minutes, until they have completely cooled.

Place 2 tablespoons butter in a large nonstick skillet over medium heat. Add mushrooms and sauté, stirring frequently, until mushroom liquid has evaporated, about 5 minutes. Place cream cheese in a large bowl. Add mushrooms, bread crumbs, chives, salt, and port wine. Stir to combine. Set aside.

Sprinkle 1 tablespoon flour on clean kitchen counter. Working with 1 puff pastry sheet at a time, place pastry on counter and roll it out to make a 14-inch square. Cut pastry into 4 equal

(7-inch) squares. Pat steaks dry with paper toweling. Place a steak in the center of each pastry square. Spread 1½ tablespoons cream cheese–mushroom mixture onto each steak. Brush 4 corners of pastry with egg wash. Fold 2 opposing corners to overlap in center of each steak. Fold the other 2 opposing corners in the same way, tucking in the sides of the pastry as if you are gift-wrapping a package. Set each pastry-covered steak on a baking sheet covered with parchment paper. Sprinkle counter with 1 tablespoon flour and repeat this process with remaining steaks and 1 more pastry sheet.

Sprinkle counter with remaining 1 tablespoon flour. Place remaining pastry sheet on counter. Cut 8 decorative shapes out of the pastry using a cookie cutter of your choice. Brush undersides with egg wash and place each atop a pastry-encased steak. Cover Wellingtons with plastic wrap and aluminum foil and refrigerate until needed. Cover egg wash and refrigerate until needed.

To serve: Preheat oven to 425°F. Brush pastry surfaces of Wellingtons with egg wash. Bake for 20 to 25 minutes, until pastry is golden. (Steaks will be medium-rare.)

Spoon a pool of warm Port Wine Sauce on each of 8 dinner plates. Place Wellingtons atop sauce. (Place remainder of sauce in a small serving bowl.) Serve immediately with Port Wine Sauce on the side.

Buy a whole beef tenderloin at your local wholesale club. Trim away fat and silver skin. Then cut tenderloin into 1¾-inch-thick steaks. Freeze remaining pieces of beef for use in kabobs or stir-fry.

Serves: 8

Grilled Dijon-Apricot Pork Medallions with Apricot-Brandy Sauce

Pork tenderloins usually come two to a package. One package should work in this recipe. You'll find the best prices at your local wholesale club.

....

¼ cup soy sauce

¼ cup apple cider vinegar

2 tablespoons brown sugar

1 tablespoon Dijon mustard

1 cup apricot spreadable fruit

2 to 2½ pounds pork tenderloin

Apricot-Brandy Sauce, heated (recipe, page 129)

....

At least 24 hours or up to 3 days ahead: Whisk soy sauce, vinegar, brown sugar, and mustard together in a small bowl. Add apricot spreadable fruit and whisk until smooth.

Place pork tenderloins in a large freezer-weight zipper bag. Pour in marinade. Close zipper and massage tenderloins until all surfaces are covered with marinade. Refrigerate until needed.

To serve: Preheat gas grill to medium temperature, about 400°F. Remove tenderloins from marinade. Place marinade in a microwave-proof bowl and microwave for 1 minute. Place tenderloins on grill and baste with reserved marinade. Grill for 3 minutes. Turn tenderloins a quarter turn and baste again with marinade. Grill for 3 minutes more. Turn tenderloins a quarter turn and baste, two more times, grilling 3 minutes each turn (total of 12 minutes grilling time). Remove tenderloins from grill and allow them to rest for 5 minutes. (Tenderloins will be medium-rare when removed from the grill. They will continue to cook to medium as they rest.) Cut into ⅜-inch medallions and serve with warm Apricot-Brandy Sauce.

....

Spreadable fruit is similar to fruit preserves, but has less sugar. Look for Smucker's or Dickinson's apricot spreadable fruit. One (9.5-ounce) jar equals about 1 cup spreadable fruit.

Serves: 6
....

Rum Marinated Grilled Pork Chops with Sweet and Sour Papaya Sauce

You can make this tasty marinade ahead and freeze it for up to one month. It is great with beef, pork tenderloin, and chicken too.

¼ cup balsamic vinegar

¼ cup spiced rum (Mount Gay or Captain Morgan)

¼ cup soy sauce

¼ cup sugar

2 teaspoons salt

1 teaspoon black pepper

2 teaspoons snipped fresh rosemary

⅔ cup chopped sweet onions, like Vidalia

4 teaspoons garlic paste or finely minced garlic

¼ cup olive oil

4 (1½-inch-thick) bone-in pork chops (about ¾ pound each)

Sweet and Sour Papaya Sauce, heated (recipe, page 136)

One day ahead: Whisk vinegar, rum, soy sauce, sugar, salt, pepper, rosemary, onions, and garlic paste together in a medium bowl. Slowly add oil, whisking constantly. Place pork chops in a large freezer-weight zipper bag. Add marinade to bag, close securely, and massage bag until pork chops are well coated. Refrigerate until needed.

To serve: Preheat gas grill on highest setting (about 500°F). Remove pork chops from marinade. Place marinade in a microwavable bowl and microwave for 1 minute. Place pork chops on hot grill. Baste with marinade. Grill for 5 minutes. Turn chops over and baste again. Cook for 5 minutes more, until pork is barely pink when tested with a sharp knife. Remove from heat (chops will continue cooking). Serve chops topped with warm Sweet and Sour Papaya Sauce.

It is important to use spiced rum in this recipe, but you can use any inexpensive balsamic vinegar. Fresh rosemary is preferable, but if you must use dried rosemary, use only 1 teaspoon.

Serves: 6

Pork and Apple Pie

This recipe is a long way from the medieval English version that called for five pounds of lard, fourteen pounds of flour, and the trimmings of a butchered hog! But in fine British tradition, sage-seasoned pork and apples are encased in flaky pastry.

....

2 tablespoons olive oil, divided

2 pounds pork tenderloin, cut into ¾-inch pieces

1 large onion, sliced, then quartered

6 ounces portobello mushrooms (2), black pith removed, halved, and sliced ¼ inch thick

3 Granny Smith apples, peeled, cored, and thinly sliced

1 tablespoon fresh lemon juice

1½ teaspoons dried sage

1½ teaspoons salt

¼ teaspoon crushed red pepper flakes

1 tablespoon Dijon mustard

1¼ cups apple juice

2 tablespoons butter

¼ cup flour

Dash ground cinnamon

1 tablespoon sugar

2 tablespoons snipped fresh flat-leaf parsley

1 rolled Pillsbury Pie Crust for 9-inch pie

1 egg, beaten with 1 tablespoon water

....

Up to 1 month ahead: Place 1 tablespoon olive oil in a large nonstick skillet over medium heat. Add pork and sauté, stirring constantly, until meat is browned on all sides. Transfer pork to a large bowl with a slotted spoon and set aside.

Wipe out skillet with paper toweling. Add 1 tablespoon olive oil. Add onions and mushrooms to hot skillet and sauté until vegetables are soft and released liquid has evaporated, about 2 minutes. Add apples and sauté 1 minute more. Add vegetables and apples to pork and mix well. Add sage, salt, red pepper flakes, and mustard to pork mixture and stir to mix well.

Microwave apple juice on high for 1 minute. Melt butter in a small saucepan over medium heat. Whisk in flour, forming a roux. Slowly whisk in warm apple juice and cinnamon, until mixture is smooth and thickened slightly. Stir apple juice sauce into pork mixture until ingredients are well coated.

....

Coat a 10-inch deep-dish pie plate with vegetable cooking spray. Transfer pork mixture to pie plate. Sprinkle with sugar, then parsley. Cover with plastic wrap, then with aluminum foil and refrigerate for up to 24 hours or freeze until needed.

To serve: Bring pie to room temperature. Preheat oven to 350°F. Allow pie crust to reach room temperature, then unroll it on a large sheet of parchment paper. Roll crust with a rolling pin until it is large enough to cover the deep-dish pie plate with a 1-inch overhang. Lift edges of parchment paper and invert crust onto pie. Crimp edges of crust and cut a 1-inch slit in the center of the crust. Brush crust and crimped edges with egg wash. Bake for 45 minutes or until crust is golden brown and pie is bubbling.

. . . .

During autumn apple season, you may want to try a different variety of apple in this dish. If you do, be sure to pick a firm cooking apple and eliminate the sugar if the apples are not particularly tart.

Serves: 8

Crusted Lamb Loaf with Tomato-Lemon Sauce

Lamb lovers will swoon over this dish. The presentation is unusual — moist lamb meatloaf surrounded with a crunchy bread crust. Pull the crust away from the lamb loaf and dip it into the Tomato-Lemon Sauce for a special treat.

....

1 (1-pound) oblong loaf sourdough bread

1 (8-ounce) can tomato sauce with basil, garlic, and oregano

½ cup chicken broth

¼ cup plus 2 tablespoons fresh lemon juice

1½ teaspoons dried oregano leaves, divided

¾ teaspoon dried thyme leaves, divided

¾ teaspoon snipped fresh rosemary, divided

2 tablespoons dark brown sugar

Coarse kosher salt

Freshly ground black pepper

1 tablespoon olive oil

5 teaspoons garlic paste or finely minced garlic

1 (8-ounce) package baby spinach, rinsed and patted dry with paper toweling

2 pounds ground lamb

2 eggs, beaten

1 (6-ounce) package basil and tomato feta cheese, crumbled

....

Early in the day or 1 day ahead: Preheat oven to 275°F. Cut the ends off the sourdough loaf and discard. Using your fingers, pull out the bread from the inside of the loaf, creating a cylindrical shell. Place shell in a zipper bag and set aside. Place the removed bread pieces on a nonstick baking sheet and bake for 10 minutes, until they dry out and start to turn golden. Remove from oven and allow to cool. Place bread in a food processor and pulse to form coarse crumbs. Set aside.

Meanwhile, make the sauce. Place tomato sauce, broth, lemon juice, ½ teaspoon oregano, ¼ teaspoon thyme, ¼ teaspoon rosemary, and brown sugar in a medium nonstick saucepan over medium heat. Season sauce with salt and pepper to taste. Bring to a boil, then reduce heat to low and simmer for 15 minutes, until sauce cooks down and thickens slightly. Transfer sauce to a covered container and refrigerate until needed.

Place 1 tablespoon olive oil in a large nonstick skillet over medium heat. Add garlic and sauté

....

for 30 seconds. Add spinach and sauté, stirring constantly, until it has wilted, about 2 minutes. Drain spinach mixture in a colander, pressing on it with the back of a large spoon to extract as much liquid as possible. Season with salt and pepper to taste and transfer spinach to a large bowl.

Add ground lamb to the skillet over medium heat. Cook lamb, stirring constantly, for just 2 minutes, until it starts to brown and release some of its grease. (Don't brown lamb completely or it will overcook.) Drain lamb in a colander and then transfer to bowl containing the spinach. Add 1 teaspoon oregano, ½ teaspoon thyme, ½ teaspoon rosemary, and ¾ cup sourdough bread crumbs. Toss to combine well. Stir in the beaten eggs and feta cheese. Season with salt and pepper to taste. Transfer to a covered container and refrigerate until needed.

One hour ahead: Preheat oven to 350°F. Stuff the lamb mixture into each end of the sourdough crust cylinder so that it is tightly packed. Place stuffed crust on a double sheet of aluminum foil and seal foil so that it can be opened from the top. Allow loaf to sit at room temperature for 15 minutes. Place foil-wrapped loaf on a baking sheet. Bake for 45 minutes. Meanwhile, warm Tomato-Lemon Sauce in a medium nonstick saucepan over low heat until it is heated through. Open foil at the top of the lamb loaf, and bake for 15 minutes more. Remove loaf from oven and allow to rest for 5 minutes. Cut loaf into ¾- to 1-inch slices and drizzle with the sauce. Serve remainder of sauce on the side.

....

😊 Place remaining sourdough bread crumbs in a freezer-weight zipper bag and freeze for use at another time.

Serves: 6 to 8

Mock Muffuletta

The famous muffuletta sandwich, or "muff," is said to have been invented in 1906 by Lupo Salvadore, who ran a little Italian market called Central Grocery on Decatur Street in the French Quarter in 1906. You'll not find an authentic "muff" outside of New Orleans.

1 (1 pound, 6 ounce) round Italian bread loaf

3 tablespoons chopped kalamata olives

3 tablespoons chopped green pimento olives

3 tablespoons chopped roasted red bell peppers

¼ cup plus 2 tablespoons chopped marinated artichoke hearts, marinade reserved

3 tablespoons olive oil

¼ pound thinly sliced turkey breast

¼ pound thinly sliced Genoa salami

¼ pound thinly sliced provolone cheese

¼ pound thinly sliced baked honey ham

¼ pound thinly sliced mortadella or bologna

¼ pound thinly sliced Swiss cheese

One day ahead: Preheat oven to 425°F. Place bread in oven, directly on oven rack, for 3 minutes, to crisp crust. Remove bread from oven. Cut bread in half horizontally. Pull crumb from the inside of both bread halves, leaving a bread shell with a 1-inch border.

Mix olives, roasted peppers, and artichoke hearts together in a small bowl. Set aside. Place bottom bread half on a dinner plate. Brush inside of both halves with olive oil.

Place a layer of turkey breast in the bottom half of the loaf (about 4 slices). Top with a layer of salami (about 5 slices), then a layer of provolone (about 3 slices). Spread one quarter of the olive mixture over the provolone. Sprinkle with 1 tablespoon reserved artichoke marinade.

Place a layer of ham atop olive mixture (about 4 slices). Top with a layer of mortadella (about 4 slices), then a layer of Swiss cheese (about 2 large slices). Place one quarter of the olive mixture atop cheese and sprinkle 1 tablespoon reserved artichoke marinade over olive mixture.

Repeat layering again in this order: turkey, salami, provolone, artichoke marinade, ham, mortadella, Swiss, olive mixture. Drizzle 1 tablespoon artichoke marinade over all. Place top bread shell over layered meats and cheeses. Place another dinner plate, upside down, atop bread. Completely cover plate-encased bread loaf with plastic wrap, tightly. Refrigerate and weight it down by placing 4 (14.5-ounce) unopened cans of soup or vegetables atop the top plate. Refrigerate overnight.

To serve: Remove can-weights and plastic wrap from muffuletta. Cut into 8 pie-shaped wedges and serve with chips and crudités.

This make-ahead sandwich is great for tailgating at a ball game or for taking along on a hike or picnic.

Serves: 8

Mango-Wasabi Tuna Steaks

Crushed dried peas and puréed mango create a yin and yang to this crusty, rare tuna steak. The wasabi adds a spicy kick while the fruit sauce cools the palate.

½ tablespoon Chinese Five Spice powder

½ tablespoon gingerroot paste or finely minced gingerroot

1 tablespoon sake

1 tablespoon ponzu sauce

2 tablespoons sesame oil

1¼ pounds yellowfin tuna steak, cut 1½-inches thick

½ pound dried wasabi peas

2 tablespoons dark brown sugar

¾ cup puréed mango, fresh or frozen and thawed

2 tablespoons butter, cut into 9 small pieces

1 tablespoon olive oil

Early in the day: Whisk together Chinese Five Spice powder, gingerroot, sake, and ponzu sauce in a small bowl. Slowly add sesame oil, whisking constantly. Rinse tuna steak, pat dry with paper toweling, and place it in a shallow container. Pour marinade over tuna. Turn tuna over several times so that it is well coated with marinade. Cover and refrigerate for 30 minutes.

Place peas in a zipper bag. Close bag and pound peas with a wooden mallet until crushed. Transfer crushed peas to a dinner plate. Crumble brown sugar over peas and mix together with clean hands.

Remove tuna from marinade and place onto bed of crumbled wasabi peas (reserve marinade). Press crushed peas onto tuna steak, covering both sides and edges thickly. Place tuna in a clean shallow container, cover, and refrigerate until needed. (Reserve crushed wasabi peas in a zipper bag and set aside.) Place reserved marinade in a medium microwave-safe bowl. Microwave for 30 seconds. Stir in puréed mango, cover, and refrigerate until needed.

To serve: Place mango sauce in a small nonstick saucepan over low heat. Simmer gently until reheated. Place olive oil in a large nonstick skillet over medium-high heat. Add tuna steak and cook each side for 30 seconds, turning with tongs. Holding steak with tongs, sear all edges. Remove steak to cutting board and cut into ⅜-inch slices. Place a pool of mango sauce on each of 4 dinner plates. Divide rare tuna steak slices into 4 equal portions and place them atop the mango sauce pool in a fan shape. Serve immediately.

Ponzu is a citrus-seasoned Japanese soy sauce that is salty, tangy, and sweet. You can substitute regular soy sauce and ½ teaspoon lemon juice for the ponzu if necessary. Wasabi is Japanese horseradish, which packs quite a wallop any time it is used. Wasabi peas are dried green peas with a spicy wasabi coating, sold as a snack food in the Asian section of most supermarkets.

Serves: 4

Mahi-Mahi Caribbean

Allow diners to open their own steaming mahi-mahi packets. Perfect for a summer out-door barbecue, the fish and trimmings can be eaten right out of the foil. For an indoor setting, guests can transfer the mahi-mahi to their dinner plates and discard the foil.

4 (4-ounce) mahi-mahi fillets

½ teaspoon salt

¼ teaspoon black pepper

2 tablespoons fresh lime juice

2 cups mashed ripe bananas (about 2 large)

½ teaspoon crushed red pepper flakes

1 tablespoon butter, softened slightly at room temperature

2 slices bacon, cut in half

2 large cloves garlic, finely minced

¼ cup chopped red onions

⅓ cup diced, peeled, seeded plum tomatoes (about 1 large)

1½ tablespoons snipped fresh basil

2 tablespoons snipped flat-leaf parsley

2 tablespoons crumbled blue cheese

Early in the day: Place mahi-mahi fillets in a single layer in a shallow container. Sprinkle with salt, pepper, and lemon juice. Cover container and refrigerate for 10 minutes. Mix mashed bananas and red pepper flakes together in a medium bowl. Set aside.

Place 4 double layers of 12-inch-square aluminum foil on kitchen counter. Spread butter liberally over the top of each. Place a half-slice bacon in the middle of each double foil. For each portion, spread 2 tablespoons mashed bananas over bacon. Place a fish fillet atop banana, then spread 2 tablespoons bananas over fillet. Sprinkle one-quarter of the garlic, onions, tomatoes, basil, and parsley onto banana for each portion. Sprinkle ½ tablespoon blue cheese over vegetables.

Close foil packets by bring lengthwise edges together and folding them over twice. Lay seam flat. Fold edges on either side over twice, forming a tightly sealed packet. Refrigerate until needed.

To serve: Preheat a gas grill to medium (400°F) or preheat oven to 400°F. Allow foil packets to reach room temperature. Place packets on grill or in oven, directly on the rack. Grill or bake for 20 to 22 minutes, until fish flakes with a fork. (Carefully open 1 packet to test.) Serve immediately, 1 packet per person.

You can use any other white fish that is ¾ to 1 inch thick. If you make the packets with thinner fillets, like snapper or tilapia, adjust the cooking time accordingly.

Serves: 4

Horseradish-Mustard-Mushroom Sauced Baked Tilapia

This easy recipe is also great with other mild-flavored white fish fillets, such as snapper, flounder, sea bass, or grouper. Adjust baking time according to the thickness of the fillets.

6 tablespoons plus 1 teaspoon butter, divided

¼ cup minced shallots

8 ounces button mushrooms, stems removed, wiped clean, and thinly sliced

3 tablespoons fresh lemon juice

3 tablespoons Dijon mustard

1 tablespoon prepared horseradish

¼ cup grated Parmesan cheese

½ cup sour cream

Salt and freshly ground black pepper

1 pound farm-raised tilapia fillets, rinsed and patted dry with paper toweling

1½ cups fresh bread crumbs

Early in the day: Melt 4 tablespoons butter in a medium nonstick skillet over medium heat. Add shallots and sauté for 1 minute. Add mushrooms and sauté for 2 minutes, stirring frequently, until mushrooms are soft. Remove from heat and set aside.

Whisk together lemon juice, mustard, horseradish, Parmesan cheese, and sour cream in a medium bowl. Add mushroom mixture and stir until ingredients are well combined. Season with salt and pepper to taste.

Grease a 9x13-inch baking dish with 1 teaspoon butter. Place tilapia fillets in a single layer in dish. Spoon mushroom sauce over fillets. Sprinkle bread crumbs evenly over sauce. Melt 2 tablespoons butter in a small glass dish in the microwave, about 20 seconds. Drizzle butter over bread crumbs. Cover baking dish with plastic wrap and refrigerate until needed.

To serve: Preheat oven to 425°F. Bring tilapia mixture to room temperature. Remove plastic wrap and bake for 15 to 20 minutes, until fish is opaque and flaky when tested with a fork.

It is important to use fresh bread crumbs in this recipe. Pulse your stale bread in a food processor until finely crumbed. Store in a zipper bag in the freezer until needed.

Serves: 4

Stuffed Flounder in Puff Pastry

Puff pastry and a spinach stuffing transform simple flounder fillets into company fare. Serve on a pool of Tomato-Caper Hollandaise Sauce.

....

1 teaspoon olive oil

5 ounces baby spinach, rinsed and patted dry with paper toweling

¼ cup chopped scallions, both white and green parts (about 2)

¼ cup roughly ground seasoned croutons

⅛ teaspoon garlic powder

½ teaspoon lemon sea salt (or ½ teaspoon coarse salt and ¼ teaspoon lemon juice)

3 tablespoons grated Parmesan cheese

1 egg, beaten

1 tablespoon flour

1 sheet frozen puff pastry, thawed in refrigerator (half a 17.25-ounce box)

2 teaspoons finely ground Italian bread crumbs

1 pound flounder fillets (2 large), rinsed and dried with paper toweling

Tomato-Caper Hollandaise Sauce, heated (recipe, page 137)

....

Early in the day: Place oil in a large nonstick skillet over medium heat. Add spinach and sauté, stirring constantly, until released liquid has evaporated. Transfer spinach to a large bowl. Add scallions, ground croutons, garlic powder, lemon sea salt, and Parmesan cheese. Stir to combine. Stir 1 tablespoon beaten egg into the mixture. Set aside.

Sprinkle flour on a clean work surface. Place puff pastry sheet on the flour. With a rolling pin, roll pastry until it measures 14x12 inches. With a pizza cutter, cut pastry into 2 pieces, each measuring 7x12 inches. Add 2 teaspoons water to remaining beaten egg. Brush each pastry half with egg wash. Sprinkle 1 teaspoon Italian bread crumbs onto each pastry half.

Place half the spinach mixture in a line down the middle of each flounder fillet, lengthwise. Roll up each fillet, jelly-roll style, starting at the short end. Place each rolled fillet, seam-side down, in the middle of a pastry rectangle, so that the length of the flounder roll lines up with the 12-inch portion of the pastry. Fold in sides of pastry, then stretch one end of pastry and then the other over flounder roll. Seal the seams and edges of pastry with an undercoating of egg wash. Brush entire surface of pastry with egg wash and place each roll on a wire rack set inside a 13x9-inch baking dish, seam-sides down. Cover with plastic wrap and aluminum foil and refrigerate until needed.

....

To serve: Preheat oven to 400°F. Remove plastic wrap and aluminum foil. Bake for 35 to 40 minutes, until pastry is golden and fish is flaky when tested with a fork. Place a pool of warm Tomato-Caper Hollandaise Sauce on each of 4 dinner plates. Cut each flounder roll in half. Top each sauce pool with pastry-encased flounder, cut-side down. Serve immediately.

Flounder fillets vary in size. The large fillets (½ pound each) roll up better around the filling and will serve 4 people, but they must be cut in half. You can also use 4 smaller fillets. Cut pastry into 4 rectangles measuring approximately 7x6 inches. Divide spinach filling into 4 portions and roll each fillet around it. Proceed with pastry wrapping described above. Reduce baking time as needed. Serve 1 pastry-encased stuffed flounder roll per person atop a pool of sauce. You can substitute sole or other thin, white fish fillets for the flounder if you like.

Serves: 4

Smoked Salmon Egg Salad

You can use this gourmet egg salad in many ways. Serve it informally as a spread with crackers. Place each serving in a butter-lettuce cup. Stuff it into toasted pita bread halves. Roll it with lettuce into a flour tortilla to form a wrap. Or fill a baked puff pastry shell for a special brunch.

....

6 large hard-boiled eggs, peeled and chopped

4 ounces smoked salmon, cut into small dice

½ cup minced red onions

2 tablespoons capers, rinsed and drained

2 tablespoons chopped fresh dill

1 tablespoon fresh lemon juice

1 teaspoon grated fresh lemon peel

½ cup mayonnaise

Salt and freshly ground black pepper

....

At least 2 hours or up to 3 days ahead: Mix eggs, salmon, onions, capers, dill, lemon juice, and grated lemon peel together in a medium bowl. Add mayonnaise and stir until ingredients are well coated and creamy. Add salt and pepper to taste. Transfer to a covered container and refrigerate until needed.

....

If smoked salmon doesn't fit your budget, you can eliminate it and still have a very tasty egg salad.

Makes: 3 cups

....

Ginger-Curried Tuna Salad

This is not your run-of-the-mill, ho-hum tuna fish salad. The unique addition of oil-sautéed curry powder and crystallized ginger transforms the ubiquitous fish spread into an Indian taste sensation.

1 teaspoon olive oil

2 teaspoons mild curry powder

½ cup mayonnaise

1 tablespoon rice vinegar

1 teaspoon Dijon mustard

¼ cup chopped red onions

3 tablespoons finely minced crystallized ginger

¼ cup finely chopped pecans

1 (12-ounce) can white tuna in water, drained, rinsed, and drained again in a colander

¼ teaspoon salt

Dash cayenne pepper

At least 1 day or up to 3 days ahead: Place olive oil in a small nonstick skillet over low heat. Add curry powder and sauté for 5 minutes, stirring frequently.

Whisk together mayonnaise, vinegar, and mustard in a medium bowl. Whisk in sautéed curry oil. Add onions, ginger, pecans, and tuna. Toss until ingredients are well combined. Season with salt and cayenne and toss again.

Transfer to a covered container and refrigerate until needed. Serve in a sandwich, in a hollowed-out tomato, or atop a bed of baby greens.

Crystallized ginger is actually strips of gingerroot that have been cooked in sugar syrup and coated with sugar. You'll find it in the spice section of your supermarket. It is most often used in baking.

Serves: 6

Greek Feta Shrimp

Traditionally made in Greece, feta cheese is salted and cured in a brine solution. Since it is naturally salty, you don't need to season the shrimp or thinly sliced tomatoes with anything but freshly ground black pepper.

1 tablespoon olive oil, divided
½ cup chopped sweet onions, like Vidalia
½ teaspoon garlic paste or
   finely minced garlic
1 cup peeled, chopped plum tomatoes
2 tablespoons chardonnay or other
   dry white wine
¼ cup snipped fresh flat-leaf parsley

¼ teaspoon salt
Freshly ground black pepper
1 pound jumbo (10/15s) shrimp,
   peeled and deveined
1 tablespoon fresh lemon juice
1 large tomato, peeled and thinly sliced
4 ounces crumbled feta cheese

Up to 1 day ahead: Place ½ tablespoon olive oil in a large nonstick skillet over medium heat. Add onions and garlic and sauté, stirring constantly, for 1 minute. Reduce heat to low. Add chopped plum tomatoes, wine, parsley, salt, and ¼ teaspoon black pepper. Cook for 5 minutes, stirring occasionally, until mixture thickens and most of the released juices have evaporated. Transfer tomato mixture to a 9x12-inch oval or 8x8-inch square baking dish that has been coated with vegetable cooking spray.

Wash and dry skillet and place it over medium heat. Add remaining ½ tablespoon olive oil. When oil is hot, add half the shrimp. Sauté, stirring constantly, until shrimp just barely turn pink. Transfer shrimp to a medium bowl. Add remaining shrimp to skillet and repeat sautéing process. Transfer shrimp to bowl and pour lemon juice over shrimp. Stir until shrimp are well coated with lemon juice.

Place shrimp in a single layer atop tomato mixture in baking dish. Pour any lemon juice left in the bowl over shrimp. Place a single layer of thinly sliced tomatoes over shrimp. Season with freshly ground black pepper to taste. Sprinkle crumbled feta evenly over sliced tomatoes. Cover with plastic wrap and aluminum foil. Refrigerate until needed.

To serve: Preheat oven to 450°F. Bring shrimp mixture to room temperature. Remove plastic wrap and foil and bake for 20 minutes, until shrimp have cooked through and mixture is bubbly. Serve with rice or orzo.

Double this recipe to serve as a dinner party entrée. Orzo is a pasta shaped like grains of barley or rice. It is very popular in Greek cuisine.

Serves: 3 to 4

Grilled Orange-Coconut Shrimp

For a quick everyday dinner, you can omit the pasta nests and skip coating the shrimp in coconut and simply serve them and the marmalade sauce atop hot spaghetti.

1 cup orange marmalade

1 cup rice vinegar

4 teaspoons garlic paste or finely minced garlic

1 teaspoon crushed red pepper flakes

1 cup sweetened flaked coconut

2 pounds jumbo (10/15s) shrimp, peeled and deveined

2 tablespoons olive oil

1 teaspoon lemon-dill or favorite seafood seasoning

8 Caramelized Onion Parmesan-Pasta Nests (recipe, page 112)

Sesame seeds

At least 1 day or up to 3 days ahead: Place marmalade, vinegar, garlic, and red pepper flakes in a small saucepan over medium heat. Bring to a boil, stirring frequently. Remove from heat and allow mixture to cool to room temperature.

Preheat oven to 400°F. Spread coconut on a nonstick baking sheet. Place in oven for 2 minutes or until coconut is toasted, stirring frequently (be careful not to burn coconut). Remove from oven and allow coconut to cool. Transfer coconut to a small zipper bag and store at room temperature until needed.

Preheat gas grill to medium-high (about 450°F). Place shrimp in a medium bowl and toss with olive oil and lemon-dill seasoning. Thread shrimp onto metal skewers, skewering through top and tail. Grill shrimp for 3 minutes per side. Remove shrimp from skewers and place in a large covered container. Pour in the marmalade sauce. Toss until shrimp are well coated with sauce. Cover and refrigerate overnight or until needed.

To serve: Preheat oven to 400°F. Place Caramelized Onion Parmesan-Pasta Nests on a nonstick baking sheet. Sprinkle with sesame seeds. Bake for 5 minutes. Turn nests over and bake for 5 minutes more.

Meanwhile, place shrimp and marmalade sauce in a medium saucepan over low heat. Heat until sauce is warm and shrimp are heated through, about 10 minutes.

Place coconut on a large plate. Remove shrimp, one at a time, from marmalade sauce and press it into coconut until shrimp is well coated. Transfer to a large plate. Place 2 pasta nests on each of 4 dinner plates. Divide shrimp into 4 equal portions and place atop pasta nests. Drizzle marmalade sauce over shrimp and pasta. Serve immediately.

If you have leftover shrimp, freeze them in the sauce and use them to top a salad or pizza. The longer the shrimp sit in the marmalade sauce, the better they taste.

Serves: 4

Coconut Crab Cakes

A taste of the islands, these spicy crab cakes are cooled by the soothing freshness of pineapple salsa. You can use prepared fresh mango salsa from the supermarket if you wish.

1 pound jumbo lump crabmeat, rinsed and drained

½ cup grated fresh coconut

⅓ cup Japanese panko bread crumbs

2 tablespoons chopped fresh flat-leaf parsley

1 teaspoon curry powder

1 teaspoon fresh lime juice

½ teaspoon gingerroot paste or grated peeled fresh gingerroot

½ teaspoon garlic paste or minced garlic

½ teaspoon minced fresh seeded jalapeño

½ teaspoon salt

¼ teaspoon ground coriander

¼ teaspoon ground cumin

¼ teaspoon cayenne pepper

2 large eggs, beaten

3 tablespoons olive oil, divided

Pineapple Salsa (recipe, page 131)

One day ahead: Place crabmeat, coconut, bread crumbs, parsley, curry powder, lime juice, gingerroot, garlic, jalapeño, salt, coriander, cumin, and cayenne pepper in a large bowl. Toss with a large spoon to mix well. Mix eggs into crab mixture with clean hands. Tightly pack crabmeat mixture into a ½-cup measure. Turn out on a baking sheet. Repeat with remaining crabmeat mixture. (You will have 6 crab cakes.) Cover baking sheet with foil and refrigerate until needed.

To serve: Preheat oven to 250°F. Place a baking sheet in oven. Place 1½ tablespoons olive oil in a large nonstick skillet over medium heat. Flatten crab cakes slightly with a spatula. Add 3 crab cakes to skillet. Sauté crab cakes, 2 to 3 minutes per side, or until golden brown. Transfer cooked crab cakes to baking sheet in oven. Add remaining 1½ tablespoons oil to skillet. Repeat process with remaining 3 crab cakes. Serve crab cakes on a bed of Pineapple Salsa.

You'll find grated fresh coconut, which is unsweetened, in the freezer section of your supermarket. Don't substitute the sweetened coconut found in the baking section. Panko bread crumbs are dried, coarse white bread crumbs.

Serves: 4 to 6

Shrimp Manicotti

Elegant and easy, this dish will conjure up the vision of a candlelit dinner on the Mediterranean shores of Italy's Amalfi coast.

1 (12-count) package dried tubular manicotti shells

1 teaspoon olive oil

1 pound small (51/60s) frozen shrimp, thawed, shelled, and deveined

⅔ cup shredded mozzarella cheese

½ cup ricotta cheese

½ cup grated Parmesan cheese, divided

1 egg, beaten

3 tablespoons snipped fresh flat leaf parsley

½ teaspoon seafood seasoning

2 cups Fresh Tomato Sauce (recipe, page 56)

One day or up to 1 month ahead: Bring a large pot of water to a boil over medium-high heat. Add manicotti shells and cook according to package instructions to al dente, about 9 minutes. Remove carefully with a large slotted spoon and place in a colander to drain. Transfer each cooked shell to a nonstick baking sheet, taking care not to rip the pasta tube.

Meanwhile, warm olive oil in a large nonstick skillet over medium heat. Add shrimp and sauté, stirring constantly, until they are just cooked through and pink, about 2 minutes. Remove from heat. Chop shrimp into small pieces and place into a large bowl. Add mozzarella and ricotta cheeses, ¼ cup Parmesan cheese, egg, parsley, and seafood seasoning. Stir until well combined.

Spread ½ cup tomato sauce in the bottom of a 7x11-inch baking dish. Using a small spoon, fill a tubular shell with shrimp mixture. Place shell atop sauce in baking dish. Repeat with remaining 11 shells. Spread remaining 1½ cups tomato sauce over stuffed manicotti shells. Sprinkle ¼ cup Parmesan cheese over sauce. Cover dish with plastic wrap, then aluminum foil, and refrigerate or freeze until needed.

To serve: Preheat oven to 350°F. Remove plastic wrap and aluminum foil. Replace aluminum foil. Bake, covered, until manicotti are hot and sauce is bubbling, about 30 to 45 minutes.

Shrimp labeled 51/60 are very small. Supermarkets quite often have great sales on this size shrimp. Look for two-for-one sales and stock up. You can substitute your favorite bottled or store-bought fresh marinara sauce if you don't have any fresh sauce in your freezer.

Serves: 6 (2 manicotti per serving)

Thai Red Curry Shrimp Enchiladas

You won't find flour tortillas in Thailand or red curry sauce in Mexico, but this fusion of cuisines accentuates the best flavors from both countries.

1 pound extra-large shrimp (16-20s), peeled and deveined
½ teaspoon lemon-herb seasoning
⅓ cup chopped red onions
⅓ cup chopped red bell peppers
⅓ cup chopped green bell peppers
½ cup chopped grape tomatoes (cut into eighths)
2 tablespoons white wine
2 teaspoons Dijon mustard
1 teaspoon dried basil
1 teaspoon dried parsley
½ teaspoon salt
½ teaspoon black pepper
2½ cups shredded Monterey Jack cheese, divided
6 burrito-size flour tortillas
1 tablespoon red curry paste
¼ cup fish sauce
2 tablespoons sugar
1 (14-ounce) can coconut milk
¼ cup snipped fresh basil

Up to 2 days ahead: Liberally coat shrimp with olive oil spray. Sprinkle with lemon-herb seasoning and toss to coat. Place a large nonstick skillet over medium heat. When hot, add shrimp and sauté, stirring constantly, until shrimp are pink and just cooked through, about 2 minutes. Transfer shrimp to a large cutting board and chop coarsely. Place chopped shrimp in a large bowl. Add onions, bell peppers, and tomatoes to bowl and toss with shrimp.

Whisk wine, mustard, basil, parsley, salt, and pepper together in a small bowl. Pour over shrimp mixture and toss until ingredients are well coated. Add 1½ cups cheese and toss to mix well.

Place tortillas on clean kitchen counter. Divide shrimp mixture evenly among tortillas (a heaping ½ cup), spreading it in the lower third of the tortilla. Fold in the sides, then fold the lower portion of each tortilla over filling, folding and wrapping until enchilada is formed. Place enchiladas, seam-sides down, in a 9x13-inch baking dish that has been coated with vegetable cooking spray. Cover dish with plastic wrap and aluminum foil and refrigerate until needed.

To serve: Preheat oven to 350°F. Allow enchiladas to reach room temperature. Whisk together red curry paste, fish sauce, sugar, and coconut milk in a medium bowl until mixture is smooth and sugar has dissolved. Uncover enchiladas and pour sauce mixture over them. Re-cover baking dish with aluminum foil and bake for 50 minutes, until sauce is bubbly. Remove foil. Sprinkle with remaining 1 cup cheese and snipped basil. Bake, uncovered, until cheese has melted, 5 to 10 minutes more. Serve 1 enchilada per person. Spoon sauce over each serving.

Fish sauce and Thai red curry paste are essential in this recipe. You can find them in the international section of your supermarket.

You can freeze leftover enchiladas and sauce in a covered container for up to 1 month. To serve, defrost and transfer them to a shallow baking dish. Cover with aluminum foil and bake at 325°F for 30 to 45 minutes, until bubbly and heated through.

Serves: 6

Scallop, Shrimp, and Artichoke Gratin

My friend Jan shared this "party perfect" recipe, for which she is held in high culinary regard in our community! Serve with a white and wild rice pilaf and a tossed salad.

1 pound sea scallops, washed and patted dry with paper toweling

1 teaspoon lemon-dill or lemon-herb seasoning, divided

2 tablespoons olive oil, divided

1 pound extra-large (16/20s) shrimp

9 tablespoons butter, divided

8 ounces button mushrooms, wiped clean with wet paper toweling and thinly sliced

1 shallot, minced

1 (13.75-ounce) can artichoke hearts in water, drained

6 tablespoons plus 2 teaspoons flour

1 cup plus 2 tablespoons milk

1 cup plus 2 tablespoons heavy cream

¼ cup plus 2 tablespoons sherry

1 tablespoon plus 1¼ teaspoons Worcestershire sauce

Salt and freshly ground black pepper

⅓ cup grated Parmesan cheese

¼ cup snipped fresh curly parsley

Up to 2 days ahead: Place scallops in a medium bowl and sprinkle with ½ teaspoon lemon-dill seasoning. Toss to combine. Place 1 tablespoon olive oil in a large nonstick skillet over medium heat. When oil is hot, add scallops and sauté, stirring frequently, for 3 minutes, until scallops have cooked through and released much of their liquid. Transfer scallops from skillet to a dinner plate with a slotted spoon and set aside. Discard cooking liquid and wipe out skillet with paper toweling.

Place shrimp in bowl and sprinkle with remaining ½ teaspoon lemon-dill seasoning. Toss to combine. Place remaining 1 tablespoon olive oil in skillet over medium heat. When oil is hot, add shrimp and sauté, stirring frequently, for 2½ minutes, until shrimp have just turned pink and start to curl. Transfer shrimp from skillet to a dinner plate with a slotted spoon and set aside. Wipe out skillet with paper toweling.

Place 2 tablespoons butter in skillet over medium heat. When butter has melted, add mushrooms and shallots. Sauté, stirring frequently, for 3 minutes, until liquid released by mushrooms has evaporated. Remove from heat and set aside.

Grease a 7x11-inch baking dish with 1 teaspoon butter. Cut artichokes in half, lengthwise, and squeeze out excess moisture. Place artichokes in an even layer in bottom of baking dish. Top with scallops, shrimp, and mushrooms. Set aside.

Place remaining butter (6 tablespoons, 2 teaspoons) in a medium nonstick saucepan over medium-low heat. When butter has melted, whisk in flour, 1 tablespoon at a time. Slowly whisk in milk and cream. Remove saucepan from heat and whisk in sherry, Worcestershire sauce, and salt and pepper to taste. Pour cream sauce over ingredients in baking dish. Sprinkle Parmesan cheese over cream sauce. Cover with plastic wrap and aluminum foil and refrigerate until needed.

To serve: Preheat oven to 375°F. Bring gratin to room temperature. Remove foil and plastic wrap. Bake gratin for 30 to 35 minutes, until heated through and bubbly. Sprinkle with parsley and serve immediately.

If you don't have or are not fond of sherry, substitute white wine. If you don't have shallots on hand, sprinkle mushrooms with onion powder to taste. Use all shrimp if you don't care for scallops.

Serves: 6

Penne Pastitsio

The Greek answer to lasagna, this dish combines savory lamb with a rich cheese béchamel sauce. It takes a bit of time to assemble but freezes well and is showy enough to be company fare.

1 tablespoon olive oil

1 cup chopped sweet onions, like Vidalia

2 teaspoons garlic paste or minced garlic

1 pound ground lamb

2½ teaspoons salt, divided

¾ teaspoon pepper, divided

2 teaspoons dried oregano leaves

¼ teaspoon ground cinnamon

1 (28-ounce) can diced tomatoes with basil, garlic, and oregano

1 (12-ounce) package multi-grain penne

6½ tablespoons butter, divided

6 tablespoons flour

2 cups heavy cream

2 cups milk

2 eggs, beaten

1⅓ cups grated Parmesan cheese, divided

⅛ teaspoon nutmeg (optional)

Up to 1 month ahead: Place oil in a large nonstick skillet over medium heat. Add onions and garlic and sauté, stirring constantly, for 1 minute. Add lamb and cook for 4 minutes, stirring frequently, until browned. Drain lamb mixture in a colander and return it to skillet. Season lamb with 1 teaspoon salt, ½ teaspoon pepper, oregano, and cinnamon. Stir in tomatoes with their juices. Reduce heat to low and simmer, uncovered, for 35 minutes, stirring occasionally.

Place a large pot of water seasoned with 1 teaspoon salt over medium heat. Cover and bring to a boil. Stir in penne. When water comes back to a boil, reduce heat to medium and cook penne for 9 to 10 minutes, until al dente. Drain penne in a colander and set aside.

Meanwhile, make béchamel sauce. Melt 6 tablespoons butter in a medium saucepan over medium heat. Gradually whisk in flour. Slowly add cream and milk, whisking constantly. Bring mixture to a boil, reduce heat to low, and cook for 3 minutes, stirring frequently. Season with

½ teaspoon salt and ¼ teaspoon pepper. Cook for 2 minutes more. Remove from burner and allow it to cool slightly, about 10 minutes. Whisk in beaten eggs and 1 cup Parmesan cheese.

To assemble: Grease a 10x10-inch or a 9x13-inch baking dish with ½ tablespoon butter. Place half the penne in the dish. Pour half the béchamel sauce over penne, spreading it evenly with the back of a spoon. Place lamb mixture in an even layer atop sauce. Place remaining penne atop lamb mixture and top with remaining béchamel sauce. Sprinkle remaining ⅓ cup Parmesan cheese and nutmeg over sauce.

Cover baking dish with plastic wrap and aluminum foil. Refrigerate or freeze until needed. Defrost to room temperature before baking.

To serve: Preheat oven to 375°F. Remove plastic wrap and aluminum foil. Re-cover dish with aluminum foil and place on a baking sheet in the oven. Bake for 45 minutes. Remove foil and bake for 15 minutes more, until golden. Allow Pastitsio to rest for 15 minutes before serving.

Freeze leftovers in a covered container. Defrost and transfer to a shallow baking dish. Cover with aluminum foil and reheat in a 325°F oven for 50 minutes or until bubbly and heated through.

Serves: 8

Tomato-Basil Tortellini

This is the perfect dinner for those days you know you'll be on the run from morning to night. Simply boil a pot of water and your meal is ready in ten minutes. The pasta sauce, assembled a day ahead, requires no cooking at all!

3 (14.5-ounce) cans petite-cut tomatoes, drained

8 ounces fresh mozzarella, cut into ¼-inch dice

¾ cup snipped fresh basil

½ cup pine nuts, dry-toasted

1 tablespoon extra-virgin olive oil

1 teaspoon garlic paste or finely minced garlic

2 teaspoons red wine vinegar

1 teaspoon salt

½ teaspoon black pepper

½ cup plus 3 tablespoons grated Parmesan cheese, divided

1 pound dry tortellini

One day ahead: Place tomatoes, mozzarella, basil, and pine nuts in a large bowl. Toss to combine. Place olive oil in a small nonstick skillet over medium heat. Add garlic and sauté for 30 seconds, stirring constantly. Stir oil and garlic into tomato mixture. Add vinegar, salt, pepper, and 3 tablespoons Parmesan cheese. Toss until ingredients are well combined. Transfer tomato mixture to a covered container and refrigerate until needed.

To serve: Remove tomato mixture from refrigerator and allow it to come to room temperature. Bring a large pot of water to a boil over high heat. Add tortellini, reduce heat to medium, and cook until al dente, following package instructions, about 10 minutes. Drain tortellini and place in a large bowl. Add tomato mixture and toss until tortellini is well coated with sauce. Spoon into individual pasta bowls and top each serving with a heaping tablespoon of Parmesan cheese. Serve immediately.

Dry tortellini is available with a variety of fillings. I used tortellini filled with sun-dried tomatoes and oregano. Any of the others — mushroom, cheese, artichoke — are equally tasty in this recipe.

Serves: 6

Artichoke-Pesto Ravioli Lasagna

If you can't find the specialty ravioli called for in this recipe, substitute an equal amount of cheese-filled ravioli. Sprinkle each ravioli layer with ¼ cup basil pesto and 2 tablespoons chopped walnuts.

1 teaspoon olive oil

1 cup chopped sweet onions, like Vidalia

1 teaspoon minced garlic or garlic paste

2 (14 .5-ounce) cans petite-cut tomatoes
with onion, celery, and peppers, drained

¼ cup diced sun-dried tomatoes

2 tablespoons snipped fresh basil

¼ teaspoon salt

1 (13.75-ounce) can artichoke hearts,
drained and chopped

1 cup shredded mozzarella cheese

1 cup ricotta cheese

1 large egg, beaten

1 (18-ounce) package frozen Rosetto Pesto
Ravioli with Walnuts (about 36 pieces)

⅓ cup shredded Parmesan cheese

Up to 1 month ahead: Heat oil in a small nonstick skillet over medium heat. Add onions and sauté for 2 minutes, stirring occasionally. Add garlic and sauté, stirring constantly, for 1 minute more. Transfer onion mixture to a large bowl. Add tomatoes, sun-dried tomatoes, basil, and salt to the onions. Stir to combine. Set aside.

Place artichoke hearts, mozzarella and ricotta cheeses, and egg in a medium bowl. Stir vigorously until well combined. Set aside.

Coat the bottom of an 8x8-inch square baking pan with vegetable cooking spray. Spread ¾ cup tomato mixture in bottom of pan. Place half the frozen ravioli squares (16 to 18) in an even layer atop tomato sauce, overlapping slightly if necessary. Spread another ¾ cup tomato sauce over ravioli. Spread half the artichoke-cheese mixture over sauce. Layer the remaining ravioli atop cheese. Top with ¾ cup tomato sauce, then the remaining cheese mixture. Spread final ¾ cup tomato sauce over cheese. Sprinkle lasagna with Parmesan cheese.

Cover with plastic wrap and aluminum foil. Refrigerate or freeze until needed.

To bake from frozen: Preheat oven to 400°F. Remove foil and plastic wrap from lasagna. Re-cover with foil. Place frozen lasagna on a baking sheet. Bake for 1½ hours or until bubbly and cooked through. Allow to rest at room temperature for 15 minutes to set up.

To bake unfrozen: If frozen, defrost lasagna. Preheat oven to 400°F. Remove foil and plastic wrap from lasagna. Re-cover with foil. Bake for 35 to 45 minutes, until bubbly and cooked through. Allow to rest at room temperature for 15 minutes to set up.

Lasagna is layered in this order: ¾ cup sauce, 16 to 18 ravioli, ¾ cup sauce, half cheese mixture, 16 to 18 ravioli, ¾ cup sauce, half cheese mixture, ¾ cup sauce, Parmesan cheese.

Serves: 4

Mushroom-Chicken Garlic-Alfredo Lasagna

This dish combines the layered goodness of lasagna with the creamy richness of Alfredo sauce.

13 tablespoons butter, divided

1 pound boneless, skinless chicken breasts, cut into bite-size pieces

¼ teaspoon dried thyme

½ teaspoon black pepper, divided

1 teaspoon crushed garlic or garlic paste

1½ pounds button, baby bella, or crimini mushrooms, sliced

1 teaspoon salt, divided

3 plum tomatoes, peeled, seeded, and diced

3 cups milk

3 (1.25-ounce) packages McCormick Creamy Garlic Alfredo Sauce Mix

1 (9-ounce) package no-cook flat-edged lasagna noodles

3 cups shredded mozzarella cheese

Up to 1 month ahead: Melt 1 tablespoon butter in a large nonstick skillet over medium heat. Add chicken, thyme, and ¼ teaspoon black pepper and sauté, stirring frequently, for 3 minutes, until chicken loses its pink color and just turns opaque. Transfer chicken to a dinner plate with a slotted spoon and set aside.

Melt 3 tablespoons butter in skillet over medium heat. Add garlic, mushrooms, ¼ teaspoon salt, and ¼ teaspoon black pepper. Sauté, stirring frequently, for 5 minutes. Add tomatoes and sauté for 5 minutes more, stirring frequently. Stir in cooked chicken. Place milk in a large nonstick saucepan over medium heat. Whisk in Alfredo sauce mix. Add remaining 9 tablespoons butter. Whisk until butter is melted and the mixture is smooth and has come to a boil. Reduce heat to low and cook for 2 minutes, whisking frequently.

Coat an 11¾x9⁵⁄₁₆x4-inch-deep, rectangular aluminum roasting pan with vegetable cooking spray. Spread ⅓ cup Alfredo sauce in a thin layer on bottom of pan. Place a layer of lasagna noodles atop sauce, slightly overlapping them. Spread ⅔ cup sauce over noodles. Using a slotted spoon, place one-third of the chicken-mushroom mixture atop sauce. Sprinkle mixture with ⅔ cup shredded cheese. Repeat layering 2 more times. Place a final layer of noodles atop cheese. Break off bits of noodles and fill in any gaps along the sides of the pan. Spread remaining Alfredo sauce over noodles and into gaps. Sprinkle remaining 1 cup cheese over lasagna. Cover lasagna pan with plastic wrap and aluminum foil. Refrigerate or freeze until needed.

To serve: Defrost lasagna, if frozen. Preheat oven to 400°F. Remove plastic wrap and aluminum foil. Re-cover with foil and bake lasagna for 45 minutes. Remove foil and bake for 15 minutes more, until lasagna is hot and bubbly. Allow lasagna to rest at room temperature for 10 minutes to firm up.

 The extra deep pan allows you to make this lasagna without sauces spilling over.

Serves: 8

Savory Brunch Cakes

These savory cakes punctuate a brunch of scrambled eggs and fresh fruit. They are also perfect for a quick breakfast on the go. Wrap heated cake in aluminum foil and take it to work with you. It tastes equally good at room temperature.

12 slices bacon, cut into ½-inch dice

¾ cup diced, peeled, seeded plum tomatoes

½ cup chopped sweet onions, like Vidalia

1 cup mayonnaise

1 tablespoon snipped fresh basil

4 ounces shredded pepper jack cheese

1 (16.3-ounce) tube Pillsbury Grands! Butter Tastin' Biscuits

Up to 1 month ahead: Preheat oven to 375°F. Place bacon in a large nonstick skillet over medium-low heat. Cook, stirring occasionally, until bacon is crisp. Remove bacon from skillet with a slotted spoon and drain on paper towels.

Place bacon in a large bowl. Add tomatoes, onions, mayonnaise, basil, and cheese. Stir until ingredients are well combined. Set aside.

Place a sheet of waxed or parchment paper on kitchen counter. Separate each biscuit dough piece into 2 pieces. Place each piece on paper and, using clean fingers, spread to double its size. Lay each piece over the cup of a regular cupcake-size, 12-count muffin pan. Press dough into bottom of cup and up the sides. Place equal portions of the tomato-bacon mixture in each of the 12 cups.

Bake for 15 to 18 minutes, until biscuits are golden and bacon mixture is bubbly. Remove from oven and cool in pan for 10 minutes. Remove cakes from pan and place on a wire rack until completely cool. Transfer to a covered container and refrigerate or freeze until needed.

To serve: Preheat oven to 325°F. (Defrost cakes in refrigerator overnight.) Place cakes, directly from refrigerator, on a baking sheet. Cover them with aluminum foil and bake for 15 minutes. Remove foil and bake for 10 minutes more, until heated through. (If cakes are at room temperature before reheating, bake for only 15 minutes or until heated through.) Serve immediately.

If you are not a fan of spicy food in the morning, substitute shredded Swiss cheese for the pepper jack.

Makes: 12 cakes (1 to 2 per person)

TBBC Gratin

Tomato, basil, Brie, and croissants, all wrapped up in a fluffy egg custard. Can brunch get any better than this? Serve this rich, decadent gratin with a fresh fruit salad.

3 plum tomatoes, thinly sliced
Salt and freshly ground black pepper
9 mini croissants
8 ounces Brie cheese, rind cut off
½ tablespoon butter
½ cup snipped fresh basil, divided
6 eggs
2 cups whole milk
¼ cup grated Parmesan cheese

One day ahead: Preheat oven to 350°F. Place tomato slices on a nonstick baking sheet. Season with salt and pepper to taste. Bake for 15 minutes. Remove from oven and allow tomatoes to cool.

Meanwhile, slice each croissant in half lengthwise, through the middle. Then cut each piece in half crosswise, so that you have 4 pieces per croissant. Set aside. Cut Brie into ½-inch dice. Set aside.

Grease a 7x11-inch baking dish with butter. Place half the croissant pieces in a layer in the bottom of the dish. Place half the Brie pieces atop the croissants. Sprinkle ¼ cup basil over Brie and croissants. Repeat each layer. Place baked tomato slices in an even layer atop gratin.

Whisk eggs in a large bowl until smooth. Add milk, ½ teaspoon salt, and ½ teaspoon pepper and whisk until well combined. Pour egg mixture evenly over tomato-topped croissants. Sprinkle Parmesan cheese over gratin. Cover with plastic wrap and aluminum foil and refrigerate until needed.

To serve: Preheat oven to 375°F. Remove plastic wrap and foil from gratin. Bake for 45 minutes, until bubbly and golden brown. Remove from oven and allow gratin to cool for 5 minutes before cutting into serving pieces.

If your household is like ours, you may not have whole milk on hand. We drink skim milk and use half-and-half in our coffee, so I use 1 cup of each in this recipe instead of the whole milk. Using all skim milk will make the egg custard too watery.

Serves: 8

Baked Vegetable Frittata

A frittata is an Italian omelet filled with bits of meat and vegetables, usually cooked on the stovetop and finished in the oven. You can substitute your choice of vegetables in this easy, all-oven, make-ahead version of the classic.

2 teaspoons olive oil, divided

½ pound spicy pork sausage links, casings removed

1 (5- to 6-ounce) bag baby spinach, rinsed and patted dry with paper toweling

½ cup finely chopped baby carrots

¾ cup chopped sweet onions, like Vidalia

8 ounces small button mushrooms, wiped clean with wet paper toweling and sliced

6 large eggs

3 teaspoons garlic paste or finely minced garlic

1 cup grated Parmesan cheese

½ teaspoon dried basil

¼ teaspoon dried marjoram

½ teaspoon salt

¼ teaspoon black pepper

1 cup shredded Jarlsberg or Swiss cheese

Up to 3 days ahead: Place 1 teaspoon oil in a large nonstick skillet over medium heat. Crumble pork sausage into skillet and cook for 2½ minutes, until browned and cooked through. Remove sausage from skillet with a slotted spoon and drain on paper toweling. Discard all but 1 teaspoon grease from skillet.

Sauté spinach in skillet over medium heat until spinach is wilted and released water has evaporated. Transfer to a dinner plate to cool.

Place 1 teaspoon oil in skillet over medium heat. Add carrots and sauté, stirring frequently, for 1 minute. Add onions and sauté, stirring frequently, for 1 minute. Add mushrooms and sauté, stirring frequently, for 1½ minutes, until water released from mushrooms has evaporated. Transfer vegetables to a large bowl. Add sausage and spinach. Stir to combine.

Place eggs in a medium bowl and whisk until smooth. Whisk in garlic, Parmesan cheese, basil, marjoram, salt, and pepper. Pour mixture into bowl with sausage and vegetables and stir until well combined. Coat a 10-inch deep-dish pie plate with olive oil spray. Pour egg mixture into pie plate. Cover with plastic wrap and aluminum foil. Refrigerate until needed.

To serve: Preheat oven to 350°F. Remove plastic wrap and aluminum foil. Sprinkle shredded Jarlsberg over frittata. Bake for 40 to 45 minutes, until a knife inserted in the center comes out clean.

You can under-bake the frittata slightly, cover it with plastic wrap and aluminum foil, and freeze it. Defrost frittata in refrigerator. To bake, remove plastic wrap and aluminum foil. Re-cover with foil and bake at 325°F for about 35 minutes, until heated through. (A knife inserted in the center will have a hot blade when frittata is heated through.)

Serves: 4 to 6

Mushroom-Bacon-Tomato Pie

This is a great brunch pie but it also makes a tasty quick supper when served with a tossed green salad.

1 (9-inch) rolled, refrigerated Pillsbury pie crust

1 pound ripe tomatoes (about 2 large)

6 slices bacon, cooked and crumbled

1 (6-ounce) jar shiitake mushrooms, drained

¼ teaspoon salt, divided

¼ teaspoon black pepper, divided

2 tablespoons snipped fresh basil, divided

½ cup sliced scallions, divided

1 cup finely shredded Swiss cheese

¾ cup half-and-half

2 large eggs

2 tablespoons flour

The day before: Preheat oven to 350°F. Using a rolling pin, roll 1 pie crust to a 10-inch diameter. Place in a 10-inch deep-dish pie pan. Crimp edges and prick bottom of crust with a fork in several places. Bake for 5 minutes. Cool for 5 minutes.

Meanwhile, core tomatoes and cut each in half horizontally. Scoop out seeds with your index finger. Cut each tomato half into thin slices. Set aside until needed.

Sprinkle bacon in the bottom of pre-baked pie crust. Sprinkle mushrooms over bacon. Place half the tomato slices in overlapping layer atop mushrooms. Sprinkle with ⅛ teaspoon salt, ⅛ teaspoon pepper, 1 tablespoon basil, and ¼ cup scallions. Repeat with remaining tomatoes, salt, pepper, basil, and scallions. Sprinkle cheese evenly over pie.

Whisk half-and-half and eggs together in a small bowl. Add flour and whisk until smooth. Pour egg mixture evenly over ingredients in pie pan. Place a 2-inch collar of aluminum foil around edges of pie crust.

Place pie pan on a baking sheet. Bake for 30 minutes. Remove from oven and cool. Remove foil collar. Cover pie with plastic wrap and aluminum foil and refrigerate until needed.

To serve: Preheat oven to 375°F. Remove plastic wrap and foil from pie. Re-cover with foil. Place pie on a baking pan. Bake for 30 minutes. Remove foil. Bake for 5 to 10 minutes more, until a knife inserted in center comes out clean.

You can freeze this cheesy pie after partially baking it for thirty minutes. Defrost to room temperature before proceeding with the final instructions.

Serves: 6 to 8

Sausage Golf Balls

These golf ball–size sausage spheres make a great pairing with a scrambled egg or French toast breakfast. Or, sandwich one in a 3-inch slider roll and take your breakfast to the golf course with you.

1 pound mild pork sausage

1 cup shredded sharp cheddar cheese

1 large egg, beaten

½ cup fresh bread crumbs

2 cups cored and peeled tart apples cut into bite-size pieces

Up to 1 month ahead: Preheat oven to 300°F. Coat a slotted broiler pan with vegetable cooking spray. Place sausage, cheese, egg, bread crumbs, and apples in a large bowl. Mix ingredients together well, using clean hands. Form mixture into 2-inch-diameter balls. Place balls on broiler pan. Bake for 35 to 40 minutes, until sausage has cooked through but is still moist. Remove from oven and allow sausage balls to cool. Place balls on a tray and place in freezer. When frozen, transfer sausage balls to a zipper bag and store them in the freezer until needed.

To serve: Defrost desired number of sausage balls and place them on a microwave-proof plate. Microwave on high for 1 minute, until heated through. Serve immediately.

Cut up into bite-size pieces, these sausage balls make a great topping for pizza.

Makes: 18 sausage balls

Sticky Rolls

Sweet, gooey, and satisfyingly rich, these easy sticky rolls are a hit any time of the day.

1 (25-ounce) package frozen Parker House or other frozen dinner rolls
½ cup chopped pecans
½ cup brown sugar
1 (3.5-ounce) package Cook 'n Serve butterscotch pudding
1 stick (½ cup) butter, melted

The night before: Coat a nonstick bundt pan with vegetable cooking spray. Place rolls at room temperature for 5 minutes so that they defrost slightly. Cut rolls in half. Layer them in the bottom and up the sides of the pan.

Sprinkle pecans onto rolls. Combine brown sugar and pudding mix in a small bowl. Sprinkle mixture evenly over rolls. Drizzle melted butter over sugar-topped rolls.

Cover pan loosely with plastic wrap and set out on counter overnight.

To serve: Preheat oven to 325°F. Remove plastic wrap. Place bundt pan in oven and bake for 40 to 45 minutes, until rolls are puffed and cooked through. Remove from oven and invert onto a serving platter. Remove bundt pan. Serve immediately.

To test if rolls are cooked through, pull one off and taste-test it. Once the bundt pan is inverted onto the serving platter, you won't notice that one roll is missing.

Serves: 8 to 10

Sides

Salads, Vegetables, Rice, and Potatoes

- Lebanese Cucumber Salad
- Citrus Splashed Spinach Salad
- Lorelei's Nine Day Coleslaw
- Med-Rim Carrot Salad
- Warm Caprese Salad
- Poppy Seed Dressed Salad in Parmesan Baskets
- Baked Parmesan Zucchini

- Tomato-Zucchini Pie
- Sweet Potato Salad
- Blueberry–Wild Rice Salad
- Fruited Chutney Rice
- Twice Baked Stuffed Potatoes
- Rice Pilaf Timbales
- Caramelized Onion Parmesan-Pasta Nests

Lebanese Cucumber Salad

It is important to use English or Persian cucumbers in this recipe. An English cucumber is about 12 inches long, wrapped in plastic, and is not waxed like regular, fat, garden-variety cucumbers. Therefore it doesn't need to be peeled. Although it is often called seedless, it does have tiny seeds that do not need to be removed. The Persian cucumber is only about 4 to 5 inches long, seedless and crunchy, and not waxed. A cucumber's seeds can emit a bitter taste, so the English and Persian cucumbers are sweeter than other varieties.

3½ to 4 cups thinly sliced, unpeeled English or Persian seedless cucumbers
1 teaspoon salt
5 tablespoons sugar
¼ cup red wine vinegar
1 tablespoon grated orange rind
¼ cup extra-virgin olive oil
2 tablespoons snipped fresh flat-leaf parsley
¼ cup snipped fresh mint

At least 2 hours or up to 2 days ahead: Place cucumber slices in a colander. Sprinkle with salt and allow cucumbers to sit for 30 minutes. Squeeze cucumbers dry with paper toweling. Place them in a medium bowl.

Place sugar in a small bowl. Whisk in vinegar. When sugar has dissolved, whisk in grated orange rind. Slowly whisk in olive oil. Pour dressing over cucumbers and toss to coat well. Add parsley and mint and toss to combine. Transfer to a covered container and refrigerate until needed.

Place cucumbers in a decorative bowl before serving.

You can also place a handful of baby salad greens on each salad plate. Place a portion of the cucumbers atop greens with a slotted spoon. Garnish with quartered grape tomatoes. Drizzle the dressing-marinade over the greens.

Serves: 8 to 10

Citrus Splashed Spinach Salad

This salad is great topped with Grilled Orange-Coconut Shrimp (recipe, page 79).

2 tablespoons fresh lime juice

3 tablespoons fresh orange juice

2 tablespoons fresh lemon juice

2 tablespoons rice vinegar

2 teaspoons gingerroot paste or finely grated peeled ginger

½ teaspoon garlic paste or finely minced garlic

3 tablespoons brown sugar

1 tablespoon sesame oil

¼ cup extra-virgin olive oil

1 (12-ounce) bag baby spinach, rinsed and dried with paper toweling

⅔ cup sliced red onions (cut into 1½-inch pieces)

1 cup sliced red and yellow bell peppers (cut into 1½-inch pieces)

1 cup chopped sugar snap peas (cut on the diagonal)

⅔ cup sliced almonds

Up to 1 week ahead: Whisk lime, orange, and lemon juices with vinegar, ginger, garlic, and brown sugar in a medium bowl. Slowly whisk in sesame oil and olive oil until emulsified. Transfer to a covered container and refrigerate until needed.

Early in the day: Prepare vegetables and almonds. Place spinach, onions, bell peppers, and sugar snap peas in a large zipper bag. Refrigerate until needed. Place almonds in a small skillet over low heat. Dry-toast until they are slightly browned. Cool and transfer almonds to a small zipper bag. Store almonds at room temperature until needed.

To serve: Bring citrus dressing to room temperature. Place vegetables and almonds in a large salad bowl. Drizzle with dressing to taste. Toss to coat ingredients well. (You will need only a portion of the dressing.)

Look for overripe citrus on sale in your supermarket. Juice it and freeze it in ice cube trays and you'll always have fresh juice on hand. You can use leftover dressing as a marinade for fish or seafood or toss it with steamed carrots or green beans.

Serves: 4 (dinner salad); 8 (side salad)

Lorelei's Nine Day Coleslaw

I lived in the Florida Keys for more than ten years, writing and tasting my way through the islands' wonderful cuisine. The Lorelei restaurant is a Florida Keys treasure, located on the Gulf of Mexico in Islamorada. Their tasty coleslaw will keep for nine days, but it usually is consumed long before that!

5 cups shredded green cabbage

5 cups shredded red cabbage

2 cups chopped onions, like Vidalia

1 yellow bell pepper, diced

2 stalks celery, diced

1½ cups plus 2 tablespoons sugar, divided

½ cup canola oil

1¼ cup cider vinegar

2 tablespoons salt

2 teaspoons celery seeds

1 teaspoon caraway seeds

Freshly ground black pepper

At least 1 day or up to 9 days ahead: Place shredded cabbage, onions, bell peppers, celery, and 1½ cups sugar in a large bowl. Toss until ingredients are well coated with sugar. Set aside.

Place 2 tablespoons sugar, canola oil, vinegar, salt, celery seeds, and caraway seeds in a medium saucepan over medium heat. Bring to a full boil, stirring constantly. Pour hot dressing over cabbage mixture and toss to combine. Season to taste with black pepper. Transfer coleslaw to a large covered container and refrigerate until needed.

To serve: Transfer coleslaw with a slotted spoon to a glass serving bowl.

Reserve dressing in the container and place any leftover coleslaw back in the container. Refrigerate until you serve it again. The slaw will remain crisp for up to 9 days.

Serves: 8 to 10

Med-Rim Carrot Salad

Countries surrounding the Mediterranean Sea are considered Med-Rim, culinarily speaking. Growers of olives and lemons, makers of fine feta cheese, and purveyors of fresh herbs and spices in the region inspire a cacophony of flavors that stimulate all of the taste buds.

1 pound baby carrots, quartered lengthwise and cut in half

½ teaspoon coarse salt

2 tablespoons minced pitted kalamata olives

3 tablespoons crumbled feta cheese

1 tablespoon snipped fresh flat-leaf parsley

1 tablespoon snipped fresh cilantro

1 tablespoon snipped fresh mint

1 tablespoon fresh lemon juice

1 teaspoon garlic paste or finely minced garlic

¼ teaspoon ground cumin

2 tablespoons extra-virgin olive oil

Freshly ground black pepper

Early in the day or up to 2 days ahead: Place a vegetable steamer and 2 inches water in a large nonstick saucepan over medium-high heat. When water comes to boil, place carrots in steamer. Steam until they can be pierced with a fork but are still crispy, about 4 minutes. Drain, rinse with cold water, and drain again. Place in a large bowl and sprinkle with coarse salt. Add olives, feta, parsley, cilantro, and mint. Toss to combine ingredients and set aside.

Whisk together lemon juice, garlic, and cumin in a small bowl. Slowly add olive oil, whisking constantly. Pour dressing over carrots and toss until all ingredients are well coated. Season carrots with black pepper to taste. Transfer to a covered container and refrigerate until needed.

To serve: Bring to room temperature before serving.

Be sure not to overcook the carrots or they will become mushy in the dressing. Check carrots for doneness every minute. Rinsing the drained carrots with cold water is imperative because it stops the cooking process and ensures the carrots remain crisp.

Serves: 4 to 6

Warm Caprese Salad

Heating the tomatoes and slightly melting the mozzarella elevates this classic salad to new heights.

1 cup fresh bread crumbs, divided
2 tablespoons grated Parmesan cheese, divided
3 ripe tomatoes, sliced ½ inch thick
Salt and freshly ground black pepper
½ knob fresh mozzarella cheese, cut into ¼-inch slices
1 tablespoon snipped fresh basil
½ tablespoon olive oil

Early in the day or up to 1 hour ahead: Coat bottom and sides of an oval gratin dish with olive oil spray. Sprinkle ½ cup bread crumbs evenly on the bottom of the dish. Sprinkle 1 tablespoon Parmesan cheese over bread crumbs.

Season tomato slices with salt and pepper. Place one tomato slice at an angle against the far side of the dish. Place one mozzarella slice against tomato slice. Repeat with all tomato and cheese slices, ending with a tomato slice. Sprinkle with snipped basil.

Sprinkle remaining ½ cup bread crumbs and 1 tablespoon Parmesan cheese over tomato and cheese slices. Drizzle olive oil onto bread crumbs.

To serve: Preheat oven to 400°F. Bake for 15 minutes. Use a small, firm spatula to serve each mozzarella-topped tomato slice.

You'll find knobs of fresh mozzarella, often packed in a watery liquid, in the deli cheese section of your supermarket.

Serves: 6

Poppy Seed Dressed Salad in Parmesan Baskets

The presentation of this salad is dramatically different from the usual humdrum side salad. And the added bonus: you can eat the basket too!

2 teaspoons minced sweet onions, like Vidalia

1 teaspoon Dijon mustard

½ teaspoon coarse salt

½ cup sugar

⅓ cup chardonnay or champagne vinegar or white balsamic vinegar

⅔ cup light olive oil

1½ tablespoons poppy seeds

2 cups shredded Parmesan cheese

4 cups mixed baby greens

1 large scallion, chopped

¼ cup diced red bell peppers

⅓ cup quartered red grapes

⅓ cup sliced almonds, dry-toasted

¼ cup crumbled feta cheese

Up to 2 weeks ahead: Place onions, mustard, salt, sugar, and vinegar in a blender. Blend at highest speed for 30 seconds. With machine on slowest speed, add oil in a drizzle, until emulsified. Add poppy seeds and blend for 10 seconds. Transfer to a covered container and refrigerate until needed. Bring to room temperature before serving. (Makes 1¼ cups.)

Early in the day: Preheat oven to 350°F. Cut four 8-inch squares out of parchment paper. Place 2 squares on each of 2 baking sheets. Place ½ cup shredded Parmesan cheese on each square and form it into an 8-inch circle with clean hands. (Make sure cheese is in a thinner layer on the edges of the circle, so that when baked the edges will look lacy.)

Bake cheese for 3 minutes. Remove parchment papers from oven and drape each, cheese-side down, over an upside-down 4-inch-diameter glass. Press paper against sides of glass to form a fluted basket. Allow cheese to cool for 20 minutes. Gently remove parchment paper and allow cheese baskets to further cool and dry, until serving time.

Early in the day: Wash baby greens and spin dry. Pat with paper towels and transfer to a zipper bag. Add chopped scallions and bell peppers to bag. Close bag and refrigerate until needed.

To serve: Place greens mixture in a large salad bowl. Add grapes, almonds, and feta cheese. Toss to combine. Toss mixture with just enough dressing to lightly coat ingredients. Remove Parmesan baskets from glasses and place each on a glass salad plate. Divide salad among baskets and serve.

The delicate baby greens fit nicely into the Parmesan baskets, but you can vary the salad by using different fruits, cheeses, nuts, and salad dressings.

Serves: 4

Baked Parmesan Zucchini

This recipe is best when made with small, young zucchini measuring about 6 to 8 inches long and 2 inches or less in diameter. Larger, older squash tend to be hard and full of seeds.

4 cups grated zucchini (about 1½ pounds)

2 teaspoons salt

¾ cup chopped sweet onions, like Vidalia

2 tablespoons snipped fresh flat-leaf parsley

¼ teaspoon dried oregano leaves

1 cup Bisquick

½ cup grated Parmesan cheese

1 teaspoon garlic paste or finely minced garlic

4 eggs

¼ cup canola oil

¼ teaspoon black pepper

Early in the day or up to 2 days ahead: Place zucchini in a large bowl. Sprinkle with salt and toss to combine. Let zucchini sit for 30 minutes. Drain in a colander. Using paper toweling, squeeze zucchini by the handfuls to release as much liquid as possible. Place squeezed zucchini back in bowl.

Add onions, parsley, oregano, Bisquick, and Parmesan cheese to zucchini in bowl. Stir until ingredients are well mixed. Set aside.

Place garlic in a medium bowl. Whisk in eggs, one at a time. Whisk in canola oil and pepper. Add egg mixture to zucchini mixture and stir until well combined.

Coat an 8x8-inch or 7x9-inch oval baking dish with vegetable cooking spray. Transfer mixture to baking dish. Cover with plastic wrap and aluminum foil. Refrigerate until needed.

To serve: Preheat oven to 350°F. Remove aluminum foil and plastic wrap. Bring zucchini to room temperature. Bake for 40 to 45 minutes, uncovered, until a knife inserted in center comes out clean.

A relative of the melon and cucumber families, the zucchini is a watery vegetable. Allowing it to sit under a sprinkling of salt for a time releases much of its inherent liquid. Squeezing it by the handfuls gets rid of this liquid and keeps the baked dish from getting soggy.

Serves: 6 to 8

Tomato-Zucchini Pie

If you'd like a cheesier pie, sprinkle the Parmesan cheese in the bottom of the crust when assembling, and substitute an equal amount of shredded cheddar cheese in the mayonnaise mixture.

¾ pound zucchini (about three 1½-inch diameter), thinly sliced

1 teaspoon salt

1 (9-inch) frozen pie crust in aluminum foil pan, thawed

4 plum tomatoes, cut into ¼-inch slices

Coarse kosher salt

Freshly ground black pepper

1 teaspoon olive oil

½ teaspoon black pepper, divided

⅓ cup grated Parmesan cheese

⅓ cup mayonnaise

½ cup snipped fresh basil

Early in the day or up to 1 day ahead: Place zucchini in a medium bowl. Sprinkle with salt and toss to combine. Let zucchini sit for 30 minutes. Drain in a colander. Using paper toweling, squeeze zucchini by the handfuls to release as much liquid as possible. Place squeezed zucchini back in bowl.

Preheat oven to 450°F. Prick bottom and sides of crust with a fork. Bake for 9 to 11 minutes, until crust has browned slightly. Remove from oven and cool on a wire rack. Reduce oven heat to 350°F. Place a sheet of parchment paper on a large baking sheet. Place tomatoes on the parchment and season with coarse salt and freshly ground black pepper to taste. Bake for 15 minutes. Remove from oven and allow tomatoes to cool.

Place olive oil in a large nonstick skillet over medium heat. Add zucchini and ¼ teaspoon pepper and sauté, stirring frequently, for 3 minutes. Transfer zucchini to a dinner plate and allow it to cool.

Mix Parmesan cheese, mayonnaise, basil, and ¼ teaspoon pepper together in a medium bowl.

To assemble pie: Place half the sautéed zucchini in the bottom of the pie crust. Place half the baked tomatoes in a layer atop zucchini. Repeat layering with remaining zucchini and tomatoes. Place teaspoonfuls of mayonnaise mixture atop tomatoes. Spread gently with the back of the spoon to form an even layer. Cover with plastic wrap and aluminum foil and refrigerate until needed.

To bake and serve: Preheat oven to 425°F. Bring pie to room temperature. Remove plastic wrap and aluminum foil. Cut or tear foil into 2-inch strips and place around edges of crust to form a protective collar. Bake for 20 to 25 minutes, until vegetables are heated through and cheese sauce is bubbly. Cut into 8 wedges and serve.

First baking the tomatoes and sweating the zucchini releases excess liquid that would otherwise make the pie soggy.

Serves: 8

Sweet Potato Salad

Sweet potatoes come in many varieties, ranging from white to yellow to orange, even red and purple. Use the orange-fleshed variety in this recipe, the flavors of which marry and intensify overnight.

4 cups peeled, diced (½-inch) sweet potatoes (2 large)

½ cup diced red onions

¼ cup dried cranberries

3 tablespoons currants

1 tablespoon Dijon mustard

2 tablespoons cider vinegar

3 tablespoons honey

2 tablespoons plus 2 teaspoons extra-virgin olive oil

½ teaspoon coarse salt

¼ teaspoon black pepper

⅓ cup chopped glazed pecans

One day ahead: Place 2 inches water in bottom of a large saucepan over medium heat. Top with a vegetable steamer. When water comes to a boil, place sweet potatoes in steamer. Cover and steam potatoes until al dente, just barely cooked through when pierced with a fork (about 6 minutes). Drain in a colander, rinse with cold water, and drain again. Place potatoes in a large covered container. Add onions, cranberries, and currants. Toss to combine.

Meanwhile, place mustard in a small bowl. Whisk in vinegar, honey, and olive oil. Pour dressing over potato mixture and toss until all ingredients are well coated. Season with salt and pepper and toss again. Cover container and refrigerate until needed.

To serve: Add pecans to salad and toss to combine. Transfer to a serving bowl and serve immediately.

You can substitute dried cherries for the cranberries, raisins for the currants, and lightly toasted unglazed pecans for the glazed pecans.

Serves: 4 to 6

Blueberry–Wild Rice Salad

Wild rice is not really a member of the rice family, being instead an annual water grass seed that grows wild in ponds and lakes of Minnesota, Wisconsin, and Canada. Laboriously harvested from boats in the open water using beating sticks that knock the grains into gathering containers, wild rice has a crunchy texture and a strong nutty flavor.

1⅓ cups water

¼ teaspoon salt

1 (2.75-ounce) box Quick Cooking Minnesota Wild Rice

1 teaspoon olive oil

1 (4-ounce) portobello mushroom, black fins scraped off, wiped clean, diced (1½ cups)

¼ cup minced shallots

3 tablespoons blueberry balsamic vinegar

1 tablespoon honey

1 teaspoon snipped fresh chives

2 tablespoons snipped fresh flat-leaf parsley

3 tablespoons walnut oil

6 tablespoon extra-virgin olive oil

1 cup fresh blueberries, washed and patted dry with paper toweling

½ cup chopped pecans

At least 1 hour or up to 4 days ahead: Place water and salt in a medium nonstick saucepan over medium heat. Bring to a boil. Stir in rice, cover, reduce heat to low, and simmer until liquid is absorbed, about 10 minutes. Fluff with a fork and transfer to a large bowl.

Place olive oil in a medium nonstick skillet over medium heat. Add mushrooms and sauté for 3 minutes, stirring constantly. Transfer to bowl with rice.

Place shallots in a medium bowl. Pour vinegar over shallots. Place honey in a small bowl and microwave for 10 seconds. Whisk honey into shallot-vinegar mixture. Whisk in chives, parsley, and the walnut and olive oils. Pour dressing over rice mixture and toss until rice and mushrooms are well coated. Transfer to a covered container and refrigerate until needed.

To serve: Bring salad to room temperature. Add blueberries and pecans and toss to combine. Transfer salad to a glass serving bowl and serve immediately.

I used Reese brand quick-cooking wild rice. If you use another brand, follow the package instructions for cooking. You can substitute plain balsamic vinegar and dried cranberries for the blueberry vinegar and fruit in this recipe. And you can use chopped walnuts instead of the pecans.

Serves: 6 to 8

Fruited Chutney Rice

Basmati rice is fragrant Indian rice with a wonderful nutty flavor. Its grains are very starchy, so the raw rice must be rinsed several times prior to cooking or the rice will stick together and not be fluffy.

1 cup basmati rice

⅓ cup raisins

¼ cup orange juice

2 tablespoons butter

½ cup finely chopped celery

⅓ cup chopped sweet onions, like Vidalia

½ tablespoon slivered orange peel

½ cup slivered almonds, dry-toasted and chopped

½ teaspoon curry powder

½ cup cranberry chutney

Salt and freshly ground black pepper

Early in the day or up to 1 month ahead: Place rice in a large, nonstick pot. Cover rice with water and, with your hands, agitate the rice, releasing the starch. Pour off the cloudy water. Repeat this process 3 times, until the water is clear. Pour off the water a final time and drain in a colander. Place rice in a large saucepan with 1½ cups water. Bring to boil, cover, and reduce heat to low. Cook for 25 to 30 minutes or until water is absorbed and rice is tender to the bite. Fluff rice with a fork and transfer to a large bowl.

Meanwhile, place raisins in a small bowl. Pour orange juice over raisins and allow them to soak for 10 minutes. Drain raisins, reserving 2 tablespoons orange juice. Set aside.

Melt butter in small nonstick skillet over medium heat. Add celery and onions and sauté for 2 minutes, until onions are soft and celery is tender. Transfer to bowl with rice.

Add raisins, reserved orange juice, orange peel, almonds, curry powder, and chutney to rice mixture. Toss to combine. Season rice mixture with salt and pepper to taste.

Coat an 8x8-inch or comparable baking dish with vegetable cooking spray. Transfer rice mixture to dish. Cover with plastic wrap and aluminum foil and refrigerate or freeze until needed.

To serve: Preheat oven to 350°F. (Defrost rice if frozen.) Remove plastic wrap and aluminum foil. Re-cover dish with foil. Bake for 20 to 30 minutes, until rice is heated through.

You will need 3 cups cooked rice for this recipe. Cooked rice freezes very well. If you have leftover cooked rice, use it in this dish.

Serves: 6

Twice-Baked Stuffed Potatoes

Serve these savory potatoes as a main course, just as they are, or top them with chili, taco meat, or shredded chicken.

3 (1-pound) Idaho baking potatoes, washed and dried

Olive oil spray

Salt

5 tablespoons butter, softened

½ cup sour cream

3 egg yolks

1 tablespoon snipped fresh chives

½ teaspoon black pepper

6 heaping tablespoons shredded sharp cheddar cheese

One day or up to 1 month ahead: Preheat oven to 375°F. Coat all surfaces of potatoes with olive oil spray and sprinkle lightly with salt. Place potatoes directly on the lower oven rack and bake for 1 to 1¼ hours, until potatoes can be easily pierced with a fork.

Cut potatoes in half lengthwise. Carefully scoop out pulp with a small spoon and place it in a large bowl. Set potato shells aside. Cut butter into 5 pieces and add to hot potatoes. Mash butter into potatoes with a fork.

Whisk sour cream, egg yolks, chives, ¾ teaspoon salt, and black pepper together in a small bowl. Mash mixture into potatoes with a fork, until well combined. Spoon mashed potato mixture into potato shells. Top each potato with a heaping tablespoon of shredded cheese. Place in a large shallow covered container and refrigerate or freeze until needed.

To serve: Preheat oven to 350°F. Bring stuffed potatoes to room temperature. Place potatoes in a large baking dish or on a baking sheet. Bake potatoes, uncovered, for 45 minutes or until heated through.

Top the potatoes with shredded Gruyère or shredded pepper jack cheese for a change of pace.

Serves: 6

Rice Pilaf Timbales

Company fare for sure, these timbales look like a work of art and taste like something you'd find at a five-star restaurant. The involved prep time is well worth the effort, because the timbales can be made ahead and frozen for up to a month. You will need 3-cup heatproof fluted molds for this recipe.

....

2 cups basmati rice

Salt and freshly ground black pepper

¼ cup canola oil, divided

2 large cloves garlic, crushed

1 tablespoon gingerroot paste or minced gingerroot

6 ounces shiitake mushrooms, stemmed, cleaned, and thinly sliced

2 tablespoons white wine

1 large sweet onion, like Vidalia, cut into quarters and thinly sliced

2 (10-ounce) bags fresh baby spinach, rinsed, dried with paper toweling, and coarsely chopped

½ cup snipped fresh curly parsley

¼ cup melted butter plus ½ tablespoon hard butter, divided

¼ cup pine nuts, dry-toasted

....

Up to 1 day ahead: Place rice in a large, nonstick pot. Cover rice with water and, with your hands, agitate the rice, releasing the starch. Pour off the cloudy water. Repeat this process 3 times, until the water is clear. Pour off the water a final time and drain in a colander. Return rice to pot and add 3 cups water and ½ teaspoon salt. Bring to a boil, uncovered, over medium heat. Reduce heat to low, cover with a tight-fitting lid, and cook for 12 minutes or until water is absorbed and rice is tender. Remove from heat, place 3 sheets of paper toweling over pot, and firmly replace lid. (Paper towels will absorb excess moisture until you are ready to use the rice.)

Place 1 tablespoon canola oil in a large nonstick skillet over medium heat. Add garlic and gingerroot and sauté for 30 seconds. Add shiitakes and stir-fry for 2 minutes, until they soften. Reduce heat to medium-low. Add white wine and cook 30 seconds longer, until wine is absorbed. Transfer mushrooms to a cutting board. Remove and discard garlic. Coarsely chop mushrooms. Add salt and pepper to taste. Set aside until needed.

Wipe out skillet and add 1 tablespoon canola oil. Place skillet over medium heat. Add onions and sauté for 10 minutes, until they are caramelized. Add salt and pepper to taste. Transfer to a dinner plate until needed.

Wipe out skillet and add 1 tablespoon canola oil. Place skillet over medium heat. Add half the chopped spinach. Stir-fry, tossing spinach constantly, until spinach is wilted, about 2 minutes. Transfer spinach to a dinner plate. Repeat process with remaining chopped spinach, transferring it to a separate plate. Season each batch of spinach with salt and pepper to taste.

To assemble: Fluff rice with a fork. Place half the rice in each of two medium bowls. To rice in one bowl add mushrooms and parsley. Toss to mix well. Add 2 tablespoons melted butter and toss to combine. Add salt and pepper to taste.

To rice in second bowl, add onions and pine nuts. Toss to mix well. Add 2 tablespoons melted butter and toss to combine. Add salt and pepper to taste.

Grease inside of two 3-cup heatproof fluted molds with hard butter. Place half the mushroom rice in each mold. Press rice firmly with a spoon, especially into the flutes. Spread one batch of sautéed spinach in each mold, pressing firmly with a spoon. Finally, place half the onion mixture in each mold, pressing rice firmly with a spoon.

Cover each mold with plastic wrap and then aluminum foil. Refrigerate one mold until needed. Freeze the other mold for up to 1 month. (Defrost it before baking.)

To serve: Preheat oven to 375°F. Remove plastic wrap and aluminum foil. Re-cover with foil and bake timbale for 20 to 30 minutes, until heated through. Remove foil and place a serving plate atop mold. Flip mold over onto plate. Remove mold and serve immediately.

....

I used a metal mold designed to shape flour tortillas into taco salad bowls, but if you don't have heatproof molds of any kind, assemble the timbales in deep-sided, 3-cup, round baking dishes and follow instructions above for unmolding.

You can use 5 cups leftover cooked rice in this recipe.

Serves: 6 to 8 (each mold)
....

Caramelized Onion Parmesan-Pasta Nests

Serve these showy pasta nests topped with Grilled Orange-Coconut Shrimp (recipe, page 79) for a dinner party entrée or fill the nests with your favorite pasta meat sauce for an everyday meal.

1 tablespoon olive oil
1 tablespoon butter
2½ teaspoons salt, divided
4 cups sliced sweet onions, like Vidalia
1 pound uncooked spaghetti
3 eggs
1 cup grated Parmesan cheese
⅓ cup snipped fresh flat-leaf parsley
Sesame seeds

Up to 1 month ahead: Place oil and butter in a large nonstick skillet over medium-low heat. When butter has melted, add onions and ½ teaspoon salt. Cover skillet and sauté onions, stirring occasionally, for 20 minutes. Uncover skillet, increase temperature to medium, and sauté for 6 to 8 minutes more, stirring frequently until onions are golden.

Meanwhile, place 2 teaspoons salt in a large pot of water. Bring to a boil over high heat. Add spaghetti, stir, and reduce heat to medium-high. Cook pasta to al dente, following package instructions, about 10 minutes. Drain spaghetti and place it in a large bowl. Cool for 10 minutes.

Place eggs in a medium bowl and beat with a wire whisk. Add onions, cheese, parsley, and beaten eggs to the spaghetti. With clean hands, toss ingredients together well.

Line several baking sheets with parchment or waxed paper. Place a 3-inch round cookie-cutter ring on the paper. Using clean hands, pack spaghetti mixture into ring. Remove ring, forming a nest. Repeat with remaining spaghetti. Place baking sheets in freezer for 1 hour, until spaghetti nests are frozen. Transfer nests to a large covered container, separating layers with parchment or waxed paper. Freeze until needed.

To serve: Defrost desired number of nests. Sprinkle with sesame seeds. Preheat oven to 400°F. Place nests on a nonstick baking sheet. Bake for 5 minutes. Turn nests over and bake for 5 minutes more before serving.

 Use whole wheat or spinach spaghetti or angel hair pasta for something different.

Makes: 21 nests

Sweets

Desserts to Die for

- English Trifle
- Peach Daiquiri Baked Alaska
- Pots de Chocolat Crème à L'Orange
- Piña Colada Rum Cake
- Strawberry-Amaretto Cheesecake
- Babycakes (2)

- Apple Galettes
- Fresh Peach Pie
- Fruit Crumble
- Old-Fashioned Gingersnap Cookies
- Freezer Cookie Logs (2)

English Trifle

An authentic English trifle is always made with Bird's Custard Powder, not always easy to find in the United States. You can order it online at www.amazon.com.

1 (3-ounce) package wild strawberry Jell-O

1 cup boiling water

1 cup pineapple juice

2 (3-ounce) packages ladyfingers

½ cup raspberry jam

1 (1-pound) package frozen sliced peaches, thawed, drained, and diced (about 2 cups)

4 cups thinly sliced fresh strawberries

2 cups fresh blueberries

2 tablespoons cream sherry

1 (2.9-ounce) package Jell-O Americana custard

2 cups whole milk or 1 cup half-and-half and 1 cup skim milk

1 cup heavy whipping cream

2 teaspoons confectioners' sugar

⅓ cup sliced almonds, dry-toasted

One day ahead: Place Jell-O powder in a medium bowl. Pour boiling water over powder and stir until dissolved. Stir in pineapple juice. Set aside to cool.

Meanwhile, separate the ladyfingers. Spread the flat side of each ladyfinger with raspberry jam. Line the sides of a large glass punch bowl or trifle bowl with the ladyfingers, jam-side in. Place a triple layer of ladyfingers in a crisscross pattern in the bottom of the bowl, jam-side up.

Place peaches atop ladyfingers in an even layer. Place strawberries in an even layer over peaches. Place blueberries atop strawberries. Sprinkle sherry over fruit. Pour Jell-O-pineapple juice mixture over fruit, allowing it to seep down into the ladyfinger layers. With the back of a large spoon, press on fruit, compressing the layers. Cover with plastic wrap and refrigerate until Jell-O is set, about 1 hour.

Meanwhile, place custard powder in a medium nonstick saucepan. Whisk in milk and place saucepan over medium heat. Whisking constantly, cook custard until it comes to a full boil, about 5 minutes. Transfer custard to a medium bowl and place a sheet of plastic wrap directly on top of custard so that no film will form. Set aside and allow custard to cool to room temperature, 30 to 45 minutes.

When custard has cooled so that it is not yet set but won't melt the Jell-O, spoon it over trifle. Cover bowl with plastic wrap and refrigerate until ready to serve.

Place whipping cream in the large bowl of an electric mixer. Beat on high until cream starts to thicken. Add sugar and continue beating until stiff peaks form. Transfer to a covered container and refrigerate until needed.

Up to 1 hour ahead: Spread whipped cream atop trifle, sprinkle with almonds, cover with plastic wrap, and refrigerate until serving.

You can make many creative substitutions in this recipe: use any in-season fruit in the same proportions; 2 teaspoons almond or banana extract for the sherry; half an angel food or pound cake for the ladyfingers; Cool Whip for the whipping cream.

Serves: 12 to 15

Peach Daiquiri Baked Alaska

Nothing is quite as showy as Baked Alaska. Slice it at the table, in full view of your guests.

1 (1½ quart) container French vanilla ice cream, softened
1 (10-ounce) can frozen peach daiquiri concentrate, thawed
4 egg whites
½ teaspoon cream of tartar
½ cup sugar

At least 2 days or up to 2 months ahead: Place ice cream and daiquiri concentrate in the large bowl of an electric mixer and mix on the lowest speed until well combined. Pour ice cream mixture into a 1-quart mold. Cover with plastic wrap and aluminum foil and place in the freezer.

At least 1 hour or up to 2 days ahead: Place a sheet of parchment paper on a wooden cutting board. Unmold ice cream mixture onto parchment. Return ice cream, on paper-covered cutting board, to freezer for 15 to 20 minutes.

Place egg whites and cream of tartar in the bowl of an electric mixer. Beat on the highest speed until egg whites are very stiff. With mixer still on highest speed, gradually add the sugar. Frost the ice cream with meringue, about ¾ inch thick. Return meringue-topped ice cream to freezer until ready to bake.

To serve: Preheat oven to 500°F. Place meringue-topped ice cream mold (still on parchment-covered cutting board) in the oven. Bake for 5 minutes, until tips of meringue have browned. Remove from oven, slice, and serve immediately.

Watch Baked Alaska carefully while it is baking. Do not overbake or the ice cream will start melting. You can substitute lemonade concentrate for the peach daiquiri concentrate for a tarter dessert.

Serves: 8 to 10

Pots de Chocolat Crème à L'Orange

A very fancy French name for a very simple, very rich, chocolaty dessert. Eggs, butter, chocolate, and orange liqueur — does it get any better than this?

6 ounces sweetened chocolate, roughly chopped into pieces
4 tablespoons butter, cut into 4 pieces
6 eggs, separated
3 tablespoons orange liqueur, like Cointreau or Grand Marnier
1 cup whipping cream, whipped with 2 tablespoons confectioners' sugar
Freshly sliced strawberries, blueberries, or raspberries

Early in the day or 1 day ahead: Bring 3 inches water to boil in the bottom of a double boiler. Place chocolate and butter in the top double boiler, cover, and melt them, stirring occasionally. Meanwhile, place egg whites in the bowl of an electric mixer and beat until stiff, about 3 minutes.

When chocolate and butter have melted, remove top of double boiler and place it on hot pad on the counter. Whisk in egg yolks, one at a time. Whisk in orange liqueur. Fold in one-third of the egg whites. Beat the remaining egg whites again until stiff and gently fold them into the chocolate mixture until well blended.

Transfer chocolate mixture to eight ½-cup serving glasses (see ⊝ below). Cover with plastic wrap and refrigerate until needed.

To serve: Remove plastic wrap from desserts. Top each with whipped cream and place glasses on small dessert dishes. Garnish with fresh berries.

⊝ Serve this dessert in parfait or champagne glasses, pots de crème cups, or small ramekins.

Serves: 8

Piña Colada Rum Cake

This is a tropical drink on a plate. Shut your eyes and your taste buds will take you to the islands.

1 (18.25-ounce) package yellow cake mix

1 (3.4-ounce) package coconut cream instant pudding mix

½ cup pineapple juice

½ cup Myers dark rum

½ cup canola oil

4 large eggs

2 tablespoons margarine or vegetable shortening

1 cup plus 2 tablespoons sugar, divided

1 cup finely chopped pecans

½ cup (1 stick) butter

¼ cup water

¼ cup coconut rum

Fresh pineapple chunks

One day ahead: Preheat oven to 325°F. Place cake mix, pudding mix, pineapple juice, dark rum, canola oil, and eggs in the large bowl of an electric mixer. Beat ingredients, scraping down sides often, for 10 minutes, until creamy and well blended.

Grease a nonstick bundt pan with margarine or shortening. Place 2 tablespoons sugar in pan. Tip pan until sugar has coated the greased pan. Sprinkle pecans in the bottom of the pan. Pour batter into the pan. Bake, uncovered, for 1 hour, until a wooden skewer inserted in the cake comes out clean. Remove cake from oven and place on a cooling rack.

Place 1 cup sugar, butter, and water in a medium saucepan over medium-high heat. Bring to a boil and boil 1 minute. Add coconut rum and boil mixture 1 minute more. Remove from heat.

Poke multiple holes in top of cake with a wooden skewer. Spoon three-quarters of the butter-rum sauce over the top of the cake. Allow cake to cool completely, about 1 hour.

When cake has cooled, reheat remaining butter-rum sauce. With a long, thin knife, carefully cut around the edges of the cake and inside the flutes of the bundt pan. Place a serving plate atop cake. Invert cake on plate. Spoon remaining warm butter rum sauce over cake. Place a glass cake dome over cake and store at room temperature until needed. Serve each slice with a skewer of fresh pineapple.

You can make this cake up to 1 month ahead and freeze it. Cut cake in quarters, wrap each quarter in plastic wrap and then aluminum foil, and freeze until needed. Thirty minutes before serving, cut a portion of frozen cake into 4 slices. Place slices on individual dessert plates, and allow them to defrost.

Serves: 16

Strawberry-Amaretto Cheesecake

Amaretto is a sweet almond-flavored liqueur. For different taste sensations, substitute other nuts for the sliced almonds and use other liqueurs, such as Cointreau or Grand Marnier.

1½ cups Nilla Wafer crumbs

⅓ cup finely chopped sliced almonds

7 tablespoons butter, divided

¾ teaspoon almond extract, divided

3 (8-ounce) packages cream cheese, softened at room temperature

Pinch salt

1 cup sugar

½ teaspoon vanilla extract

1 cup sour cream

3 large eggs

⅓ cup Amaretto

Strawberry Coulis (recipe, page 134)

16 unhulled strawberries, rinsed, dried, and sliced to the hull

At least 1 day or up to 1 week ahead: Preheat oven to 350°F. Mix wafer crumbs and almonds together in a medium bowl. Melt 6 tablespoons butter in a small dish in the microwave. Add melted butter and ¼ teaspoon almond extract to crumbs. Mix together with a fork. Grease the sides of an 8-inch springform pan with remaining tablespoon butter. Place crumbs in pan and press them evenly on bottom and slightly up the sides of pan. (Make sure the bottom of the pan is firmly covered in crumbs.) Bake crust for 10 minutes. Remove crust and allow it to cool.

Meanwhile, place cream cheese in the bowl of an electric mixer. Beat until smooth. Add salt, sugar, vanilla, and ½ teaspoon almond extract. Beat until smooth. Add sour cream and beat for 3 minutes. (Mixture should be very creamy.) Beat in eggs, one at a time. With mixer at low speed, stir in Amaretto until well mixed.

Pour cream cheese mixture into cooled crust. Place springform pan on a baking sheet and bake for 1 hour. Turn off heat, prop open oven door 2 or 3 inches, and allow cheesecake to cool for 3 hours. Trim off any cake that might have oozed over the sides of the pan. Cover cheesecake pan with plastic wrap and aluminum foil and refrigerate overnight.

To serve: Remove plastic wrap, foil, and sides of springform pan. Place Strawberry Coulis in a plastic squeeze bottle. Drizzle a decorative design on each dessert plate. Slice cheesecake and place slices atop coulis-decorated plates. Drizzle coulis over each serving of cheesecake and top each with a sliced strawberry fan.

You can freeze this cheesecake for up to 1 month. Pre-cut slices before freezing. Defrost slices in the refrigerator for several hours before serving.

Serves: 16

Babycakes

Babycakes are the ultimate make-ahead dessert. These individual cakes, baked in maxi muffin pans, are frozen until needed, then defrosted on dessert plates for a mere 30 minutes.

KEY LIME GLAZED BABYCAKES

1 (18.25-ounce) Duncan Hines Moist
   Deluxe Lemon Supreme cake mix
1 (3.4-ounce) package lemon instant pudding
4 large eggs
½ cup water

½ cup canola oil
¾ cup Key lime juice, divided
2 cups confectioners' sugar, sifted
Strawberry Coulis (recipe, page 134)

Preheat oven to 350°F. Place cake mix, pudding mix, eggs, water, canola oil, and ½ cup Key lime juice in the bowl of an electric mixer. Beat until creamy, about 2 minutes, scraping down the sides occasionally. Place paper liners in cups of 2 maxi muffin pans (6-count). Spoon batter into paper liners, filling them just over half full. Bake for 17 to 18 minutes, or until an inserted wooden skewer comes out clean.

Remove muffin pans from oven. Pulling gently on the paper liners, remove cakes from pans and allow them to cool on a wire rack for 3 minutes. Remove paper liners from cakes and transfer babycakes to a baking sheet lined with parchment paper or waxed paper.

Whisk together confectioners' sugar and ¼ cup Key lime juice in a medium bowl. Using a wooden skewer, make about 8 puncture holes in the top of each babycake. Drizzle an equal amount of lime-sugar mixture over the top of each warm cake with a spoon, allowing excess to run down the sides. With a table knife or small frosting spatula, spread the pooled lime-sugar mixture up the sides of each cake and drizzle excess over the top until glaze hardens.

Transfer cakes to large covered containers lined with parchment paper or waxed paper. Freeze cakes until needed.

Thirty minutes before serving: Place individual cakes on dessert plates and allow them to defrost.

To serve: Place Strawberry Coulis in a plastic squeeze bottle. Drizzle sauce decoratively on plates and atop each babycake.

Don't substitute Persian lime juice in this recipe. The cakes will be too sweet. Nellie & Joe's brand bottled Key lime juice is available in many supermarkets. Go to their Web site (www.keylimejuice.com) to find a list of online retailers and supermarkets carrying their product. The bottled juice does have a shelf life once opened. Freeze it in ½-cup portions; frozen juice keeps forever.

Serves: 10

CLASSIC CARROT BABYCAKES

3 cups flour

2 teaspoons baking soda

¼ teaspoon salt

1 teaspoon ground cinnamon

3 large eggs

2 cups sugar

1½ cups canola oil

3 teaspoons vanilla extract, divided

1 (16-ounce) can crushed pineapple
    with juices

2 cups grated raw carrots

1 cup finely chopped walnuts

1 (1-pound) box confectioners' sugar

¼ cup (4 tablespoons) butter,
    softened at room temperature

1 (8-ounce) package cream cheese,
    softened at room temperature

Up to 1 month ahead: Preheat oven to 350°F. Sift together flour, baking soda, salt, and cinnamon. Set aside. Beat eggs in the large bowl of an electric mixer. Add sugar and beat until well combined. Add oil and beat until frothy.

Add flour mixture, several tablespoons at a time, beating on medium speed and scraping down sides of bowl often. Add 1 teaspoon vanilla, pineapple, carrots, and walnuts. Beat on low speed until well combined.

Place paper liners in cups of 2 maxi-muffin pans (6-count). Spoon batter into paper liners, filling them about three-quarters full. Bake for 30 minutes or until an inserted wooden skewer comes out clean. (Repeat with remaining batter.)

While cakes are baking, make the cream cheese frosting. Place confectioners' sugar, butter, cream cheese, and 2 teaspoons vanilla in the large bowl of an electric mixer. Beat until creamy.

Remove cakes from oven. Pulling gently on the paper liners, remove cakes from muffin pans and allow them to cool on a wire rack for 5 minutes. Remove paper liners from cakes and transfer cakes to baking sheets lined with parchment paper or waxed paper. Cool for 10 minutes more.

Frost tops and sides of each babycake with cream cheese frosting. Place baking sheets in freezer and freeze cakes until firm, about 2 hours. Transfer cakes to large covered containers lined with parchment or waxed paper. Freeze cakes until needed.

Thirty minutes before serving: Place individual cakes on dessert plates and allow them to defrost.

🕙 Carrot cake is especially good in the autumn. Top the babycakes with a garnish of candy corn, minced candied pineapple, or finely chopped walnuts.

Serves: 15

Apple Galettes

A galette is a flat, pancakelike French pastry often topped with fresh fruit. Demerara cane sugar is raw, unrefined sugar whose crystals are coarse and light golden brown. It tastes more like real sugar cane than white refined sugar.

1 cup orange juice

4 Fuji apples or other sweet-tart apples

2 (17.3-ounce) boxes frozen puff pastry sheets, defrosted in refrigerator (4 sheets)

5 tablespoons demerara cane sugar or regular white sugar, divided

4 tablespoons apricot jam

1½ tablespoons water

French vanilla ice cream

Up to 2 days ahead: Preheat oven to 400°F. Place orange juice in a large bowl. Working with 1 apple at a time, peel, core, and cut it into thin slices. Immediately submerge apple slices in orange juice to keep them from turning brown.

Working with 1 sheet of puff pastry at a time, cut 5-inch-diameter circles with a cookie or biscuit cutter, or use a similar-size saucer as a template. Place each circle of pastry on a baking sheet lined with parchment paper and prick with a fork about 6 times. (You'll get 2 circles of pastry per sheet.) Place remaining puff pastry in a zipper bag to keep it moist, and set it aside (see below).

Remove apple slices from juice with a slotted spoon. Place apple slices in a slightly overlapping circle atop pastry so that they resemble petals of a flower. Sprinkle each galette with ½ teaspoon sugar. Bake galettes for 20 minutes, until edges of pastry are puffed and golden. Remove from oven and allow galettes to cool for about 3 minutes.

Mix jam and water together in a small bowl, breaking up any large chunks of apricot. Brush each galette liberally with apricot mixture, then allow galettes to cool completely. Refrigerate in a covered container until needed.

To serve: Bring galettes to room temperature. Place 1 galette on each dessert plate. Place a small ball of ice cream in the center of each and serve immediately.

Use leftover apples and pastry scraps to make apple tartlets. Cut remaining apple slices in half. Form remaining puff pastry dough in a ball and roll it out into a large sheet about ¼ inch thick. Use a 3-inch-diameter round cookie cutter to cut small circles out of the pastry. Place pastry circles on parchment paper–lined baking sheet. Top each with sliced apples and sprinkle with ¼ teaspoon sugar. Bake for 15 to 18 minutes. Brush each tartlet with apricot mixture. Makes about 15 tarts. Refrigerate in a covered container until needed.

Serves: 8

Fresh Peach Pie

The sweet, unadulterated flavor of fresh peaches shines through in this easy, make-ahead pie. Take advantage of fresh peach season by freezing filling for multiple pies, which you can enjoy all year long. You will need a 10-inch-diameter aluminum foil pie pan.

1½ cups sugar

2 tablespoons cornstarch

3 tablespoons Minute Tapioca

9 to 10 fresh freestone peaches

1 (15-ounce) package rolled Pillsbury Pie Crusts (2 crusts)

Up to 3 months ahead: Mix sugar, cornstarch, and tapioca together in a medium bowl. Set aside.

Bring a medium saucepan of water to boil over high heat. Remove pan from heat and place on a hot pad. Place each peach in hot water for about 30 seconds. Remove peaches from water and peel each one. Slice each peach and put slices in a large bowl. Add sugar mixture and toss until peaches are well coated. You will need about 6 cups sliced peaches.

Place two large pieces of aluminum foil inside a 10-inch aluminum pie pan, pressing so that foil conforms to pie pan. Transfer peach mixture to pie pan. Cover with a double layer of foil and crimp edges securely. Place in freezer until needed.

To serve: Preheat oven to 450°F. Remove pie pan from freezer. Remove foil-lined peach filling from pan. Roll out 1 pie crust to fit the 10-inch-diameter pie pan. Trim bottom crust around pan edge. Remove all foil from peach filling and place frozen filling into pie crust. Roll out second crust and place atop filling. Wrap excess crust under edge of bottom crust. Crimp edges. Cut 4 or 5 slits in the top crust.

Place pie on a baking sheet. Cut aluminum foil into 2-inch strips. Place strips around edges of crust to form a protective collar. (This will keep edges from overcooking.) Bake for 20 minutes. Reduce heat to 350°F. Bake for 50 minutes more. Remove foil collars from crust and bake 25 to 30 minutes longer, until pie is bubbly and crust is golden. Allow to cool for at least 15 minutes before serving.

Substitute an equal amount of fresh sliced strawberries, blueberries, blackberries, or peeled, cored, sliced apples for the peaches whenever these fruits are in season.

Serves: 8

Fruit Crumble

You can use any combination of fruits in this easy, make-ahead crumble. You'll need seven cups of fruit. Fresh cranberries are a nice addition in the autumn, fresh berries in the summer months.

½ teaspoon ground cinnamon
⅓ cup plus ¼ cup dark brown sugar
½ cup flour, divided
3 pears
3 tart apples
2 peaches
½ cup quick or old-fashioned rolled oats

¼ teaspoon baking powder
¼ teaspoon salt
1½ tablespoons canola oil
1 tablespoon apple juice
Cool Whip, whipped cream, frozen vanilla
   yogurt, or vanilla ice cream

One day or up to 1 month ahead: Place cinnamon, ⅓ cup brown sugar, and 2 tablespoons flour in a large bowl. Set aside.

Peel, core, and cut pears and apples in quarters, lengthwise. Slice quarters, crosswise, into ½-inch pieces. Toss with brown sugar mixture.

Peel, seed, and slice peaches. Cut slices into bite-size pieces. Toss with brown sugar mixture.

Coat an 8x8-inch-square glass baking dish with vegetable cooking spray. Transfer fruit mixture to dish. Set aside.

Combine oats, ¼ cup brown sugar, remaining 6 tablespoons flour, baking powder, and salt in a medium bowl. Mix oil and apple juice together in a small bowl and sprinkle the liquid over oats mixture. Mix with clean fingers until crumbly. Sprinkle crumb mixture evenly atop fruit mixture.

Cover with plastic wrap and then aluminum foil. Refrigerate or freeze until needed.

To serve: Defrost Fruit Crumble if frozen. Preheat oven to 350°F. Remove plastic wrap and aluminum foil. Bake for 40 minutes, until topping is brown and filling is bubbly. Remove from oven and place on a wire rack to cool slightly, about 5 minutes. Spoon crumble into individual bowls. Top warm crumble with Cool Whip, whipped cream, frozen vanilla yogurt, or vanilla ice cream.

During the winter months, when fresh fruit is not as readily available as in other seasons, substitute a combination of frozen fruits and berries. You don't need to defrost the frozen fruit before assembling the crumble, but add 2 more tablespoons flour to the cinnamon, flour, and brown sugar mixture that you toss with the fruit.

Serves: 6 to 8

Old-Fashioned Gingersnap Cookies

Some things get better with age! These classic cookies taste best when several days old.

2 cups flour

2 teaspoons baking soda

1 teaspoon ground cinnamon

½ teaspoon ground cloves

½ teaspoon ground ginger

½ teaspoon salt

¾ cup (1½ sticks) margarine, softened at room temperature

1½ cups sugar, divided

¼ cup molasses

1 egg

At least 2 days ahead: Sift flour, baking soda, cinnamon, cloves, ginger, and salt together in a medium bowl. Set aside.

Place margarine and 1 cup sugar in the bowl of an electric mixer and beat until well mixed. Add molasses and egg and beat until creamy. With electric mixer at low speed, add flour mixture, several spoonfuls at a time. Beat until smooth and creamy. Cover bowl with plastic wrap and refrigerate for 2 to 3 hours.

To serve: Preheat oven to 375°F. Place ½ cup sugar on a dinner plate. Using clean hands, roll dough into 1-inch balls, then roll balls in sugar. Place sugar-coated balls on a parchment paper–lined or greased baking sheet about 2 inches apart. Bake for 10 to 12 minutes, until golden brown and crackled. Remove from oven and allow cookies to cool for about 2 minutes on the baking sheet. Transfer cookies to a wire rack with a thin spatula and allow them to cool completely. Store in an airtight container at room temperature or freeze until needed.

These cookies remind me of those my grandmother used to make. They store well at room temperature, but you can make them ahead and freeze them until needed. Serve with French vanilla ice cream for a quick and easy dessert.

Makes: 45 cookies

Freezer Cookie Logs

Make up the dough for these cookies when the spirit moves you, then freeze the dough in logs. Bake as many cookies as you want, whenever you want, in mere minutes. Simply cut frozen slices and bake. Each recipe makes about four dozen cookies.

CRANBERRY-PECAN-OATMEAL SCONES

Not conventional scones, but these nutritious cookies make good breakfast dunkers.

2 cups flour

½ tablespoon baking powder

1 teaspoon coarse salt

2 sticks unsalted butter, softened at room temperature

1 cup sugar

1 large egg

¼ cup sour cream

2 cups quick oats

1 cup dried cranberries

½ cup pecan pieces or chopped pecans

Up to 1 month ahead: Sift flour, baking powder, and salt onto a dinner plate. Set aside. Place butter and sugar in the bowl of an electric mixer and beat until smooth, about 2 minutes. Add egg and beat until light and fluffy, about 1 minute. Scrape down sides of bowl and beat in sour cream. Beat in flour mixture, about 3 heaping kitchen tablespoons at a time, scraping down sides of bowl after each addition. With mixer on low speed, fold in oats, cranberries, and pecans.

Place 2 sheets of plastic wrap (each about 16 inches long) onto the counter. Divide dough between the sheets, forming a 14-inch line on each. Fold one long side of each plastic wrap over dough and roll up, folding in the ends. Massage the rolls of dough into 14-inch logs. Cover each log with a second piece of plastic wrap. Place in the freezer for up to 1 month.

To serve: Preheat oven to 350°F. Place a sheet of parchment paper on a baking sheet. Run hot water over a paring knife. Cut cookie logs into ½-inch slices and place on parchment paper. Bake for 14 minutes or until golden.

Makes: 4 dozen scones

CURRANT-PISTACHIO-BUTTERSCOTCH-CHOCOLATE CHIP COOKIES

These are the go-to treats when you need a cookies-and-milk fix before bedtime.

2½ cups flour

1 teaspoon baking soda

1 teaspoon coarse salt

2 sticks unsalted butter, softened at room temperature

½ cup sugar

¾ cup dark brown sugar, firmly packed

2 large eggs

2 teaspoons vanilla extract

1 cup semisweet chocolate chips

1 cup butterscotch chips

½ cup dried currants

⅓ cup finely chopped pistachios

Up to 1 month ahead: Sift flour, baking soda, and salt into a small bowl. Set aside.

Place butter, sugar, and brown sugar in the bowl of an electric mixer and beat until well creamed, about 2 minutes. Add eggs, one at a time, beating each about 30 seconds, until incorporated. Scrape down sides of bowl and beat in vanilla extract. Beat in flour mixture, about 3 heaping kitchen tablespoons at a time, scraping down sides of bowl after each addition. With mixer on low speed, fold in chocolate and butterscotch chips, currants, and pistachios.

Follow instructions in previous recipe for forming dough into logs, freezing, and baking.

Makes: 4 dozen cookies

Extras

Sauces and Salsa

- Apricot-Brandy Sauce
- Peanut-Coconut Sauce
- Pineapple Salsa
- Plum-Ginger Sauce
- Port Wine Sauce

- Strawberry Coulis
- Sweet Garlic Sauce
- Sweet and Sour Papaya Sauce
- Tomato-Caper Hollandaise Sauce

Apricot-Brandy Sauce

Serve this piquant sauce with Grilled Dijon-Apricot Pork Medallions (recipe, page 64) or plain grilled pork chops, boneless chicken breasts, or steak.

2 tablespoons light brown sugar, divided

1¼ cups (two 5.5-ounce cans) apricot nectar

2 tablespoons beef broth

½ cup plus 2 tablespoons brandy

2 teaspoons minced garlic or garlic paste

1 teaspoon dried marjoram

½ cup chopped sweet onions, like Vidalia

2 tablespoons fresh lemon juice

1 tablespoon cornstarch dissolved in 1 tablespoon water

½ cup finely chopped dried apricots

Up to 3 days ahead: Place brown sugar, apricot nectar, broth, brandy, garlic, marjoram, onions, and lemon juice in a medium nonstick saucepan over high heat. Bring to a boil, stirring constantly. Reduce heat to medium-low and simmer for 2 minutes, stirring constantly. Transfer sauce to a blender and puree for 30 seconds. Return sauce to pan and reduce heat to low. Add dissolved cornstarch and cook for 2 minutes, stirring constantly. Add dried apricots and cook for 2 minutes more, stirring constantly. Transfer sauce to a covered container. Cool, uncovered, in refrigerator for 10 minutes. Cover and refrigerate until needed.

To serve: Place sauce in a medium nonstick saucepan over medium-low heat. Cook, stirring frequently, for about 3 minutes, until sauce has heated through.

 You can freeze sauce for up to 1 month.

Makes: 2¼ cups

Peanut-Coconut Sauce

Serve this sauce with Chicken Strudels (recipe, page 38) or Two-Way Satay (recipe, page 61).

½ teaspoon canola oil

½ teaspoon garlic paste or finely minced garlic

¼ cup chopped sweet onions, like Vidalia

½ cup chopped unsalted peanuts

1 teaspoon finely chopped red chilies with seeds

2 teaspoons brown sugar

1 teaspoon fresh lime juice

⅔ cup coconut milk

1 teaspoon soy sauce

Up to 2 days ahead: Place oil in a small nonstick saucepan over medium heat. Add garlic and onions and sauté, stirring constantly, for 1 minute. Add peanuts and sauté, stirring frequently, for 1 minute more. Remove saucepan from heat. Stir in chilies, brown sugar, lime juice, coconut milk, and soy sauce. Transfer to a covered container and refrigerate until needed.

To serve: Reheat in microwave for 1 minute.

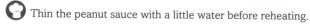
Thin the peanut sauce with a little water before reheating.

Makes: ¾ cup

Pineapple Salsa

Serve salsa with Chicken Tikka Kabobs (recipe, page 40) or Coconut Crab Cakes (recipe, page 80).

1 cup finely diced fresh pineapple
½ cup finely diced red bell peppers
½ cup finely diced green bell peppers
½ cup finely diced red onions
4 scallions, green parts only, chopped
2 tablespoons snipped fresh cilantro
2 teaspoons fresh lemon juice
½ teaspoon fish sauce
1 tablespoon honey
2 teaspoons extra-virgin olive oil
Freshly ground black pepper

At least 12 hours or up to 2 days ahead: Place pineapple, bell peppers, red onions, scallions, and cilantro in a medium container. Whisk together lemon juice, fish sauce, and honey in a small bowl. Whisk in olive oil. Pour dressing over salsa ingredients and toss until ingredients are well coated. Season to taste with freshly ground black pepper. Cover container and refrigerate until needed.

Fish sauce is a pungent, salty liquid made from fresh anchovies. Essential in Thai cooking, it is used in Southeast Asia as we would use soy sauce or table salt.

Makes: 2¾ cups

Plum-Ginger Sauce

Serve this piquant sauce with Asian Shrimp Bites (recipe, page 20), Chinese Chicken Cups (recipe, page 27), or Chicken Strudels (recipe, page 38).

⅔ cup bottled plum sauce

¼ cup thinly sliced scallions

3 tablespoons soy sauce

2 tablespoons rice vinegar

1 tablespoon gingerroot paste or finely grated gingerroot

1 tablespoon honey

Up to 2 days ahead: Whisk together plum sauce, scallions, soy sauce, vinegar, gingerroot, and honey in a medium bowl. Cover and refrigerate until needed or freeze in small covered containers. Allow sauce to reach room temperature before serving.

Sometimes called duck sauce, bottled plum sauce is a sweet sauce with a fruity ginger flavor made from plum puree, gingerroot, sugar, and vinegar. You'll find it in the Asian section of your supermarket.

Makes: 1 cup

Port Wine Sauce

Serve sauce with Individual Wellington Mignons (recipe, page 62) or simply grilled filet mignon steaks.

2 tablespoons butter, divided
½ cup chopped sweet onions, like Vidalia
1 teaspoon garlic paste or finely minced garlic
1 tablespoon tomato paste
½ cup port wine
2 cups beef broth
1 tablespoon cornstarch whisked with 1 tablespoon water
2 tablespoons red currant jelly

Up to 1 week ahead: Melt 1 tablespoon butter in a medium nonstick saucepan over medium heat. Add onions, garlic, and tomato paste. Cook for 1 minute, stirring constantly. Add port wine. Cook for 2 minutes, stirring frequently. Add beef broth. Reduce heat to medium-low and simmer for 10 minutes, stirring occasionally. Pour sauce through a strainer. Place in a covered container and refrigerate until needed or freeze for up to 1 month.

To serve: Place sauce in a small nonstick saucepan over high heat. Bring to a boil. Reduce heat to low. Stir in cornstarch mixture. When sauce has thickened slightly, stir in currant jelly and remaining 1 tablespoon butter.

Port wine, a sweet, dark-red dessert wine originally from Portugal, is essential in this recipe. Sipping-quality port wine is quite expensive, but you can purchase cheaper varieties suitable for cooking.

Makes: About 2 cups

Strawberry Coulis

Coulis is a thick sauce made with pureed fruit. Serve with Strawberry-Amaretto Cheesecake (recipe, page 119) or Key Lime Glazed Babycakes (recipe, page 120).

3 cups (1 pound) sliced fresh strawberries

6 tablespoons plus 1 teaspoon confectioners' sugar, divided

2 tablespoons peach schnapps

Up to 1 month ahead: Place strawberries and 2 tablespoons confectioners' sugar in a blender. Pulse until strawberries are roughly pureed. Add remaining confectioners' sugar and pulse to combine. Add schnapps and blend until smooth. Divide coulis equally between 2 covered containers. Refrigerate for up to 1 week or freeze for up to 1 month.

One hour ahead: If coulis is frozen, defrost at room temperature until needed.

Place in a plastic squeeze bottle to drizzle onto desserts or ice cream.

Makes: 2¼ cups

Sweet Garlic Sauce

Serve sauce with Two-Way Satay (recipe, page 61) or serve with plain grilled pork chops, boneless chicken breasts, or steak.

2 tablespoons garlic paste or finely minced garlic
½ teaspoon Asian sweet chili sauce
½ cup brown sugar
½ cup rice vinegar
⅔ cup water

Up to 1 week ahead: Place garlic, chili sauce, brown sugar, vinegar, and water in a small nonstick saucepan over medium-low heat. Whisk to combine. Bring to a boil, reduce heat to low, and simmer for 15 to 17 minutes, until mixture has reduced to about half. Remove from heat. Transfer to a covered container and refrigerate until needed.

To serve: Reheat in microwave for 1 minute.

 You can find sweet chili sauce in the international foods section of your supermarket.

Makes: ¾ cup

Sweet and Sour Papaya Sauce

Serve sauce with Chicken Strudels (recipe, page 38) or Rum Marinated Grilled Pork Chops (recipe, page 65).

3 tablespoons butter

2 tablespoons brown sugar

½ cup pineapple juice

1 teaspoon soy sauce

¼ cup apple cider vinegar

½ teaspoon grenadine

1 tablespoon cornstarch

½ cup chicken broth

½ cup finely diced fresh papaya

¼ cup finely chopped bottled roasted red bell peppers

Up to 3 days ahead: Melt butter in a medium nonstick saucepan over medium heat. Add brown sugar and stir until sugar is dissolved. Whisk in pineapple juice, soy sauce, vinegar, and grenadine. Place cornstarch in a small bowl. Whisk in chicken broth. Add to ingredients in saucepan and whisk until mixture thickens, about 5 minutes. Remove from heat and stir in papaya and roasted red peppers. Transfer to a covered container and refrigerate until needed.

To serve: Place sauce in a medium nonstick saucepan over low heat. Reheat sauce, stirring occasionally, until it is heated through, 3 to 4 minutes.

Papayas are green when you buy them in the supermarket. Ripen them at room temperature until they are yellow and appear to be pockmarked with rotten spots. (This indicates they are ripe.) Cut open, scoop out the black seeds and save or discard them. (Papaya seeds are the source of commercial meat tenderizers and are great in homemade marinades.) Peel the papaya and cut the bright orange flesh into bite-size pieces. Papaya can be stored in a covered container in the refrigerator for up to a week. If you don't like papaya or don't have one on hand, you can substitute fresh or frozen finely diced peaches in this recipe.

Grenadine is a red syrup flavored with pomegranates, commonly used in mixed drinks.

Makes: 1 cup

Tomato-Caper Hollandaise Sauce

Serve this tangy sauce atop Chicken Saltimbocca Roulades (recipe, page 45) or with Stuffed Flounder in Puff Pastry (recipe, page 74).

6 tablespoons butter, divided

1 cup water

1 (1.25-ounce) package McCormick Hollandaise Sauce Mix

2 tablespoons fresh lemon juice

1½ teaspoons sugar

¾ cup dry white wine

¼ cup thinly sliced scallions (about 1 large)

¾ cup diced (½ inch) seeded plum tomatoes

3 tablespoons capers, rinsed and drained

Early in the day or 1 day ahead: Melt 4 tablespoons butter in a medium saucepan over medium-low heat. Add 1 cup water and sauce mix. Whisk until well mixed. Cook sauce, whisking frequently, until it comes to a boil. Reduce heat to low and simmer for 1 minute, whisking constantly, until thickened.

Remove sauce from heat. Whisk in lemon juice, sugar, and wine. Stir in scallions, tomatoes, and capers. Transfer to a covered container and refrigerate until needed.

To serve: Place sauce in a medium nonstick saucepan over low heat. Cut 2 tablespoons butter into 9 small pieces. Add butter to sauce. Simmer sauce for 10 minutes, stirring occasionally. Serve immediately.

If you use a different hollandaise sauce mix, follow package instructions. Use a good white wine, not cooking wine, in this recipe.

Makes: 1½ cups

Effortlessly placing a hot, nutritious meal on your family's table in minutes, night after night, may seem an unattainable sleight of hand. Magicians rarely reveal the secrets to their illusions, but in culinary circles we know it is what goes on behind the scenes, ahead of time, that counts. With a well-stocked pantry, the right equipment, a handful of innovative tips, and a little pay-it-forward time, you'll be able to create gustatory magic.

STOCKING THE PANTRY, 'FRIDGE, AND FREEZER

Pantry

PRODUCE
bananas

garlic

onions: sweet onions like Vidalia, red onions

potatoes: Idaho baking

shallots

tomatoes: slicing, grape, plum or Roma

BAKING SUPPLIES
baking powder

baking soda

Bisquick

butterscotch chips

chocolate: sweetened, semisweet chips

cornstarch

Crisco

extracts: vanilla, almond

flour (all-purpose)

Minute Tapioca

Quaker Quick 1-Minute or Old-fashioned Rolled Oats

sugar: granulated white, confectioners', light brown, dark brown, demerara

SEASONINGS AND MIXES
bread crumbs (dried): panko, Italian seasoned

broth and stock: beef, chicken, vegetable, College Inn Thai Coconut Curry broth

cake mixes: yellow, lemon supreme

dried fruits: cranberries, apricots, raisins, currants

jams/jellies/marmalades: orange marmalade, red currant jelly, mango chutney, cranberry chutney, apricot preserves or spreadable fruit, seedless raspberry preserves

Jell-O: strawberry

Jell-O pudding: Cook 'n Serve butterscotch, Americana custard, coconut cream custard, lemon instant

Liquid Smoke

nuts: salted and unsalted peanuts, glazed pecans, wasabi peas

pepper: cracked black pepper, freshly ground black pepper, white pepper, crushed red pepper flakes, cayenne

red curry paste

salt: kosher or coarse salt, table salt, lemon sea salt

sauce mixes: Creamy Garlic Alfredo Sauce, Hollandaise Sauce, Béarnaise Sauce (McCormick), Knorr Alfredo mix

spices: allspice, basil, bay leaves, caraway seeds, celery seed, chili powder, chipotle chile powder, Chinese Five Spice seasoning, cinnamon (ground, sticks), citrus grill seasoning (Durkee's), cloves (ground, whole), coriander (ground, seeds), cream of tartar, cumin, curry powder (mild Sharwood's or Madras), dry mustard, garlic powder, ginger (ground, crystallized), Greek seasoning (Penzeys), Italian seasoning (Penzeys), lemon-dill seasoning, lemon-herb seasoning, lemongrass, marjoram, nutmeg, onion powder, oregano, poppy seeds, red chilies (dried), sabzitorshi herbs, sage, seafood seasoning, seasoning salt, sesame seeds (white and black), thyme

sun-dried tomatoes: whole, julienne-cut

MISCELLANEOUS
almond syrup (orgeat)

Angostura Bitters

bottled water

coconut: sweetened, flaked

corn tortillas

croutons (seasoned)

flour tortillas: 10-inch

ginger ale

grenadine

juices: apple, cranberry, pineapple

Knox gelatin

ladyfingers

liquor: white wine, red wine, port wine, sherry, sake, Grand Marnier, rum (coconut, Myers dark, white, spiced), gin, Amaretto, brandy, Crème de Cocoa, Jack Daniel's whiskey, peach schnapps

nectars: apricot, guava, peach, mango

Nilla Wafers

pasta: penne, multi-grain penne, no-cook flat lasagna noodles, manicotti shells, spaghetti, dried tortellini

pizza crusts (Mama Mary's Gourmet Pizza Thin & Crispy Crusts)

rice: basmati, quick-cooking Minnesota Wild Rice

tea bags

CANNED GOODS
artichoke hearts: plain, marinated

coconut milk: light, regular

pineapple: chunks, crushed

red salmon

soup: Campbell's Tomato Bisque

tomato paste: with basil, garlic, and oregano

tomato sauce: with basil, garlic, and oregano (See *Behind the Magic* section, page 145)

tomatoes (diced): with basil, garlic, and oregano (See *Behind the Magic* section, page 145)

tomatoes (petite-cut): unseasoned; in garlic and olive oil; with onion, celery, and peppers

tuna (white)

water chestnuts

JAR OR BOTTLED GOODS

Asian sweet chili sauce

Busha Brown's Pepper Sherry

capers

fish sauce

honey

hot sauce or Tabasco sauce

hoisin sauce

ketchup

mayonnaise

molasses

mustard: Dijon, fruit-flavored honey mustard, Vidalia onion mustard

oils: olive, extra-virgin olive, canola, olive oil spray, vegetable oil spray, toasted sesame, walnut

olives: pimento-stuffed green, kalamata

pasta sauce: tomato and basil, sweet basil marinara, spicy marinara

pesto: basil, sun-dried tomato

plum sauce

ponzu sauce

roasted red bell peppers

salsa (chunky)

shiitake mushrooms

soy sauce

vinegars: red wine, champagne, rice, cider, balsamic, white balsamic, blueberry balsamic

wasabi mayonnaise

Worcestershire sauce

Freezer

BREADS

breads and rolls: mini croissants, oblong sourdough, round Italian, Parkerhouse, ready-to-bake baguette

STAPLE INGREDIENTS

Athens Mini Fillo Shells

bread crumbs, fresh *(See Behind the Magic section, page 144)*

butter *(See Behind the Magic section, page 145)*

cheese: (shredded, crumbled) blue, sharp cheddar, mozzarella, plain feta, tomato-basil feta

citrus zest: orange, lemon *(See Behind the Magic section, page 145)*

fruits: sliced peaches, raspberries, unsweetened coconut

herbs: snipped flat-leaf parsley, basil, rosemary, cilantro, chives, thyme, mint, curly parsley, dill *(See Behind the Magic section, page 144)*

ice cream: French vanilla

juices: (fresh) lemon, lime, orange, Key lime; (concentrates) orange, lemon, limeade, peach daiquiri *(See Behind the Magic section, page 145)*

nuts: almonds (sliced, slivered), pine nuts, pecans, walnuts, roasted pistachios *(See Behind the Magic section, page 144)*

phyllo (fillo) dough

pie crusts: deep-dish in foil pan, Pillsbury 9-inch rolled crusts

puff pastry

ravioli (Rosetto Pesto Ravioli with Walnuts)

MEAT, SEAFOOD, AND POULTRY

beef: lean ground, sirloin steak cut 1¼ inches thick, flank steak, filet mignon steaks, tenderloin tidbits

chicken: boneless, skinless breasts

duck: boneless breasts

lamb: ground

pork: bone-in chops, tenderloins, ground

sausage (pork) spicy links, mild bulk; (turkey) sweet, hot Italian

shrimp (uncooked, shell on): 10/15s, 16/20s, 31/40s, 51/60s

turkey: ground

Refrigerator
....

PRODUCE

apples (sweet tart)

avocado

bell peppers: red, yellow, green

berries: blueberries, strawberries, cranberries

cabbage: green, red

cantaloupe

carrots: baby, shredded, whole

celery

chile peppers (jalapeño)

citrus: oranges, lemons, limes

cucumber (English)

eggplants

garlic

gingerroot

grapes (red)

herbs: (whole) mint, flat-leaf parsley, basil

juices: orange, lemon, lime, apple cider
(See Behind the Magic section, page 145)

leafy greens: baby spinach, mixed baby greens

leeks

mushrooms (fresh): white button, baby bella, Portobello, shiitake

papaya

peaches

pears

pineapple

scallions

sugar snap peas

sweet potatoes

watermelon

Yukon Gold potatoes (These potatoes have a higher sugar content than other potatoes. Store them in a paper bag or perforated plastic bag in crisper drawer of refrigerator.)

zucchini

DAIRY

butter: salted, unsalted

cheese (chunk): mozzarella, miniature mozzarella balls, sharp yellow cheddar, extra-sharp white cheddar, pepper jack, Brie, Swiss, Monterey Jack, Gruyère, Boursin

cheese (sliced): provolone

cream cheese: whipped cream cheese, sun-dried tomato and basil flavored, plain

eggs (large)

half-and-half

heavy whipping cream

margarine

milk: whole, skim

Parmesan cheese: grated, shredded

ricotta cheese (part-skim)

sour cream

yogurt (plain)

MEAT, SEAFOOD, AND POULTRY

bacon (center-cut)

cold cuts: turkey breast, Genoa salami, baked honey ham, mortadella or bologna, prosciutto

crabmeat (jumbo lump)

fish: yellowfin tuna steaks cut 1½ inches thick, smoked salmon, flounder, mahi-mahi, tilapia

imitation seafood (pollock): crabmeat, lobster

MISCELLANEOUS

biscuits: Pillsbury Grands! Butter Tastin' Biscuits, Pillsbury Grands! Junior Flaky Biscuits

guacamole

herb pastes: garlic, gingerroot *(See Behind the Magic section, page 144)*

horseradish (prepared)

pizza crust (Pillsbury)

wonton wrappers

Equipment and Supplies

- **Special bakeware:** You'll need a nonstick bundt pan for Sticky Rolls and for Piña Colada Rum Cake; 12-count regular muffin pan for Savory Brunch Cakes; three (6-count) maxi muffin pans for Babycakes; mini muffin pans for Meatballs Four Ways; 8-inch springform pan for Strawberry-Amaretto Cheesecake.

- **Assembly molds and equipment:** You'll need a 5½-cup decorative shrimp or fish mold for the Shrimp Mousse; 3-inch round cookie cutter for the Caramelized-Onion Parmesan-Pasta Nests; 5-inch round cookie cutter for Apple Galettes; two (3-cup) fluted molds for Rice Pilaf Timbales; four (4-inch-diameter) glasses for Parmesan Nests (Poppy Seed Dressed Salad); 4-inch wooden skewers for Cocktail Skewers; metal skewers for Chicken-Tikka Kabobs, Two-Way Satay, and Grilled Orange-Coconut Shrimp (seafood will stay in place better if metal skewers have flat shafts instead of round); 24-count mini muffin pan for Faux Seafood Biscuit Baskets; large glass punch bowl or trifle bowl for English Trifle; 1-quart mold for Peach Daiquiri Baked Alaska; plastic squeeze bottle for Strawberry Coulis; 1½-cup bowl for Major Grey's Chutney-Curry Spread.

- **Special serving items:** Recipes specify eight (½-cup) glasses for Pots de Chocolat Crème à L'Orange; 6 small crystal glasses for Chilled Chocolate-Almond Soup and Iced Tomato-Melon Soup; 8 champagne glasses and 8 long-handled spoons for Chilled Zucchini Soup; 6 martini glasses for Fresh Herbed Cucumber-Yogurt Soup.

- **Aluminum baking pans:** You'll need an 11¾x9⁵⁄₁₆ x 4-inch deep, rectangular aluminum roasting pan for the Mushroom-Chicken Garlic-Alfredo Lasagna; 10-inch aluminum foil pie pan for Fresh Peach Pie.

- **Other pans you'll need:** Broiler pan, nonstick skillets and saucepans (small, medium, large), soup pot, deep sauté pan, baking sheets, 10-inch deep-dish pie plate, baking pans (7x11-inch, 9x13-inch, 8x8-inch, 10x10-inch, 7x9-inch oval, 9x12-inch oval), double boiler for Pots de Chocolat.

- **Cooking oil pump sprayer:** Misto is a popular brand found at most stores that sell kitchen supplies. Light olive oil or canola oil works best in the sprayer. Using real cooking oil is more economical; allows for a more even, controllable spray; and is free of the chemicals commonly found in commercial aerosol cooking sprays.

- **Two sets of measuring cups:** You need one set of measuring cups for liquids (1-cup, 2-cup, and/or 4-cup glass or plastic calibrated in ounces) and one set for measuring dry ingredients (1 cup, ½ cup, ⅓ cup, ¼ cup). Level dry ingredients with a knife.

- **Parchment paper:** You can substitute butcher paper or waxed paper for parchment paper when flash-freezing items, but don't make such a substitution when baking. You do not have to grease a baking sheet if you line it with parchment paper.

- **Microplane grater:** One of a cook's best investments is an ultra-sharp microplane grater, available at most stores that sell kitchenware (about $15). You can grate lemon, lime, or orange peel in mere seconds. You can finely grate gingerroot, garlic, onion, or even chocolate.

BEHIND THE MAGIC

- You'll never have to mince garlic or grate gingerroot again when you use pastes from Gourmet Gardens (in the produce section of your supermarket). The finely ground herb pastes last for months and eliminate prep time mincing, chopping, and snipping. I always keep the garlic and gingerroot paste in my refrigerator, but the company also makes red chilli pepper, cilantro, basil, and lemongrass pastes as well. The cost is about 19 cents a tablespoon. The pastes are real time-savers.

- A well-stocked spice collection is a must. Mine actually inhabits several shelves of my pantry. Spices, however, can be expensive, especially when you may use the seasonings infrequently. I buy my spices from www.penzeys.com. The company sells an exceptionally wide range of fresh spices in small quantities at reasonable prices. They have retail stores in only a handful of cities in the U.S., but they offer a complete color catalog as well as a great Web site for ordering through the Internet.

- The other essential flavor weapon in my arsenal is a freezer full of fresh herbs, snipped and flash-frozen. I buy bundles of fresh herbs when they are inexpensive and plentiful in the summer season: curly and flat-leaf parsley, basil, rosemary, cilantro, chives, thyme, oregano, mint, and dill. I turn on the television, grab a pair of kitchen scissors, and snip the herbs (rinsed and spun-dry) into a bowl as I watch the news or a movie. Then I transfer the herbs to individual zipper bags, label, and freeze them. Frozen herbs will keep in the freezer for a year, are easy to measure, and add a jolt of flavor freshness that dried herbs simply can't provide. (If you must resort to using dried herbs, use one-third to one-half the amount of fresh herbs, depending upon the age of the dried herbs. Dried herbs lose their potency over time.)

- I find that fresh bread crumbs work much better in a lot of recipes than dried crumbs. I put my odds and ends of bread in the food processor (don't worry if they are different types of breads), process them until they are fine-grained, then transfer them to a freezer-weight zipper bag that I keep in the freezer. The bread crumbs will keep up to a year.

- Storing buns and rolls in the freezer guarantees you'll have what you'll need for a quick sandwich. So often, however, frozen bread and rolls get freezer-burned and turn dry and tasteless. It takes a little more time, but I have found that wrapping individual buns and rolls in plastic wrap before freezing and then placing them in a freezer-weight zipper bag keeps them bakery-fresh once defrosted.

- I think the addition of dried fruits or chopped nuts gives a flavor boost to lots of dishes. While dried fruits can be kept almost indefinitely in the pantry, only a few roasted nuts, like peanuts and cashews, should be stored this way. I keep bags of chopped walnuts, pecans, macadamia nuts, pistachios, pine nuts, and sliced almonds in my freezer so they don't become rancid. Place them in a small nonstick skillet over low heat and dry-toast them before adding them to salads or sprinkling over cooked food as a garnish. If you are using them in a recipe, you can use them frozen.

- Fresh citrus juices and grated peel are essential elements in my cooking. My supermarket — and probably yours too — sells bags of "overripe" oranges, limes, and lemons for a fraction of the price usually charged for these expensive fruits. (A mere eighty-nine cents usually nets me six or seven lemons.) If the peel is still unblemished, I grate the citrus with a microplaner (see Equipment and Supplies list) and then freeze it in a labeled zipper bag. The juice is still good, so I squeeze the citrus and freeze the juice in small plastic containers. I also keep small bottles of lemon juice and lime juice in the refrigerator at all times. If a recipe calls for a tablespoon of fresh lemon juice, it is at my fingertips.

- Many recipes call for just a tablespoon of tomato paste or a quarter cup of tomato sauce or even a small amount of pesto. I wrap the unused portion of tomato paste in plastic wrap, forming a cigar-shaped roll, and freeze it. When I need another tablespoon of paste, I simply unroll the plastic wrap and cut off what I need with a sharp paring knife. I freeze extra tomato sauce and pesto in an ice cube tray and store the cubes in labeled zipper bags. I store unused chicken, beef, and vegetable broth in ½-cup plastic containers in the freezer. They defrost in the microwave in seconds. Waste not, want not!

- Homemade soup is far superior to the canned varieties, both in taste and nutritional values. But a pot full of soup can last for days. Who wants to eat the same soup every day for a week? Here is the quick, easy answer: Freeze extra soup and chili in maxi muffin tins. Each muffin cup holds 1 cup of soup. Pop frozen soup out of the muffin cups and store them in labeled freezer-weight zipper bags in the freezer. When you want a cup of soup, place a frozen soup block in a microwave-safe bowl, then defrost and reheat it. This is also a convenient way to take lunch to work: Place a block of soup in a covered microwave-safe container. Take it to work with you and allow the soup to defrost at room temperature all morning. By lunchtime, the soup will be defrosted and you can reheat it in the microwave. Easy, tasty, and inexpensive!

- Butter freezes very well. I always buy several pounds when I find it on sale and keep it on hand in the freezer, defrosting and using it stick by stick. Butter comes salted and unsalted. When butter is called for in the recipes in this book, use salted butter. (I indicate when unsalted butter is required, usually in baking.) Salt is added as a preservative that is not needed as long as you keep your butter refrigerated, so if all you have is unsalted butter, add ¼ teaspoon salt per ½ cup butter when salted butter is indicated.

- I always like to use sweet onions, such as Vidalia or Walla Walla, in my recipes. These onions have a higher sugar content than Spanish yellow onions, so they are not as strong-tasting, and they have a mild, sweet flavor. Because of the higher sugar content, however, they don't store as long as other onions. Keep them refrigerated and buy only the amount you'd use within two weeks time. On the other hand, shallots — distant cousins of the onion — store well for months in the refrigerator. Very important in most cuisines of the world, shallots have a mild flavor with a hint of garlic. If a recipe calls for shallots and you don't have them, use an equal amount of chopped onions and add a finely minced clove of garlic.

Food Facts Revealed

- **How do you tell if eggs are fresh?** Examine the data stamped on the carton! Two dates are printed on egg cartons: One is the "sell by" date. The other is a 9-digit number called the Julian date, the last three numbers of which indicate the day of the year the eggs were packed. For instance: 097 would be April 7, the 97th day of the year. For the eggs to be fresh, the "sell by" date should be no more than 30 days after the Julian date. Eggs with a Julian date closest to the purchase date will be the freshest.

- **How much juice is in a piece of citrus?** A medium-sized lemon or lime will yield about 2 tablespoons juice and 2 teaspoons grated peel. You'll get about ¼ cup juice from a Valencia (juice) orange and about 1 tablespoon grated peel. A greenish tinge on a Valencia orange does not mean it is unripe. The oranges sometimes "re-green" in warm weather.

- **Why do recipes often call for garlic in different forms?** Whether the peeled garlic is whole, sliced, chopped, minced, or smashed dictates the intensity of the flavor. Whole cloves are the mildest. And if you bake them in their peels, they will spread like butter. The garlicky flavor imparted to the food gets stronger the more the garlic clove is cut: sliced = mild; chopped = medium; minced = full flavor; smashed = intense.

- **How do you thicken soup?** Whisk together 1 tablespoon cornstarch with 2 tablespoons cold water for each 2 quarts of clear broth soup. For a pureed vegetable soup, flour the vegetables before cooking or add a handful of peeled, diced potatoes to the soup. Or you could add ½ cup cooked rice or beans or a slice of bread sautéed in olive oil to the soup before blending. A splash of cream or a dollop of yogurt will thicken soups as well. It is best to add these ingredients to the soup after you take it off the burner so that they don't curdle.

- **What's the best way to thaw frozen shrimp?** If you have time (all day), let them defrost in the bag in the refrigerator. If you are short on time, place the bag of frozen shrimp in a large bowl of cold water for an hour. For a really speedy thaw, place the bag of shrimp in a bowl of warm water for 15 minutes, changing the water every 5 minutes. The big no-no? Don't let thawed shrimp sit at room temperature. Refrigerate them until needed.

- **Why is saffron so expensive and what is the best way to maximize its impact on cuisine?** The stigma of the fall-flowering crocus, which is harvested by hand, saffron commands thousands of dollars per pound. Only 5 to 7 pounds of saffron can be harvested from each acre of land. Indian saffron from Kashmir is considered the best in the world, but Spanish saffron is more widely available and less expensive (about $9 to $10/gram). Luckily, a little goes a long way. Rub several threads of saffron between your fingers and place in a small cup of warm liquid, such as water, wine, or broth that will be used in your recipe. Allow saffron to steep for about 20 minutes. The liquid will turn yellow. Add the infused liquid to the other recipe ingredients.

- **Is there a difference in measurements between "1 cup flour, sifted" and "1 cup sifted flour?"** You bet! Sifting aerates the flour, giving it more volume, so "1 cup flour, sifted" will actually be more than a cup of flour if you measure it after you sift it.

- **Why do recipes say to "allow meat to rest at room temperature for 5 minutes" once it is taken off the grill or out of the oven?** First, the meat will continue to cook once it is removed from the heat, so you have probably removed it before it was quite done. Secondly, cooking causes the juices to move from the edges to the center of the meat. When allowed to rest off-heat, the juices redistribute themselves so the entire piece becomes juicier.

- **Many recipes specify different kinds of vinegar. Is there really a difference in the flavor?** Red wine vinegars commonly found in the supermarket are made from Concord grape juice and are fairly sweet. If you find one that is made from cabernet or merlot, it will be more expensive, more complex, and tarter. Similarly, white wine vinegar is made from white grapes. Champagne and chardonnay vinegar — types of white wine vinegar – are more difficult to find, are more subtly flavored, and, of course, are more expensive. A favorite home brew for centuries, apple cider vinegar is a flavorful pantry staple, great in cooked recipes. A fine balsamic vinegar is like a great bottle of port wine. It can cost $40 or more. Use it in small droplets atop a mozzarella and tomato salad or drizzle it over grilled fish. Don't waste it on a tossed salad. A lot of inexpensive vinegars sold as balsamic are actually red wine vinegar in disguise. Invest in a medium-grade balsamic, which will cost about $15, to use for everyday salads and marinades. Rice vinegar, light and mild-flavored, is commonly used in Asian cuisine. That said, you'll notice a flavor difference in vinegars when they are used in fresh salad dressings, but if you need a tablespoon or two in a recipe, any vinegar will do.

TABLE OF EQUIVALENTS

Some of the conversions in these lists have been slightly rounded for measuring convenience.

VOLUME:		OVEN TEMPERATURE:	
U.S.	metric	fahrenheit	celsius
¼ teaspoon	1.25 milliliters	250	120
½ teaspoon	2.5 milliliters	275	140
¾ teaspoon	3.75 milliliters	300	150
1 teaspoon	5 milliliters	325	160
1 tablespoon (3 teaspoons)	15 milliliters	350	180
2 tablespoons	30 milliliters	375	190
3 tablespoons	45 milliliters	400	200
1 fluid ounce (2 tablespoons)	30 milliliters	425	220
¼ cup	60 milliliters	450	230
⅛ cup	80 milliliters	475	240
½ cup	120 milliliters	500	260
⅔ cup	160 milliliters		
1 cup	240 milliliters		
2 cups (1 pint)	480 milliliters		
4 cups (1 quart or 32 ounces)	960 milliliters		
1 gallon (4 quarts)	3.8 liters		

WEIGHT:	
U.S.	metric
1 ounce (by weight)	28 grams
1 pound	448 grams
2.2 pounds	1 kilogram

LENGTH:	
U.S.	metric
⅛ inch	3 millimeters
¼ inch	6 millimeters
½ inch	12 millimeters
1 inch	2.5 centimeters

INDEX

Acknowledgments

Just as for the past six books I have written, the refrain remains the same: "I get by with a little help from my friends!" My most patient critic and chief guinea pig, my husband Bob, and my most loyal taste-testers — Vivienne and Frank Afshari, Bill and Sue Hendrick, Suzanne and John Tobey, Linda and Jim McGaan, Ola Lilley, Randy and Susie Williams, and the Monday Bridge Club gals — stayed true to their commitment: "You make it, we'll eat it!" Your courage was admirable and your input invaluable.

And to those folks who augmented the scores of recipes I developed by sharing some of their personal treasures: Shirley Grahek, Linda McGaan, Melanie Winter, Margit Donaldson, Barbara Geesey, Linda Visscher, Bob Adams, Jan Brown, and Sue Shaffer — thank you, thank you, thank you!

To the person who keeps me in the kitchen and has made this cookbook series possible, Megan Hiller at Sellers Publishing, thanks for believing in me once again. I so enjoy working with you.

And of course, along with my hubby, thanks to my family: the Rochester Shearers — Brian, Lisa, Bethany, Bobby, and Leia; the Raleigh Wingenbachs — Kristen, John, Ashleigh, Christopher, and Nicholas; and the Florida golden girls — mother June Harbort and aunt Fern Miller. Always hungry and game to try anything, you all helped make this book possible.